THE FRENCH HOMEBUYER'S GUIDE

A Step-by-Step Path to Your Dream House in France

Alistair McLeod

ISBN: 9798325378072

DISCLAIMER

This guidebook provides general insights about purchasing a house in France, but is not a substitute for professional legal, financial, or real estate advice. The information is educational and requires the reader to consult professionals before making property-related decisions. Despite the author and publisher's efforts to ensure the information's accuracy and completeness, they cannot guarantee its applicability in all situations nor be held liable for errors, omissions, or consequences of its use.

The reader is responsible for staying informed of changes in laws, regulations, and market conditions related to French property ownership. The reader's decisions and actions related to buying a house in France are their sole responsibility, and the author and publisher assume no liability for any negative outcomes resulting from the application of the information contained in this guidebook.

CONTENTS

INTRODUCTION

Welcome to "The French Homebuyer's Guide," penned by Alistair McLeod, an experienced expert in international property ownership. This guide will support your journey towards owning a home in France, an enchanting country with diverse appeal. The process of home-buying in a foreign country can be daunting due to unfamiliar language, legal systems, and cultural norms, but this guide simplifies it with real-life examples and practical advice.

You'll be walked through the home-buying process in France, from understanding the real estate market and the financial aspects to navigating the French legal framework. Furthermore, you'll gain insights into property search, negotiation, and finalizing the sale, as well as settling into your new life in France.

This comprehensive guide aims to equip you to navigate the French property market confidently, helping you to find your dream home.

I: UNDERSTANDING THE FRENCH REAL ESTATE MARKET

Before diving into the process of buying a home in France, it's crucial to familiarize yourself with the French real estate market. Understanding the unique aspects of the market, including regional variations, property types, and market trends, can help you make informed decisions and ultimately find the perfect property to suit your needs and budget. In this section, we'll explore some key aspects of the French real estate market that every prospective buyer should be aware of.

REGIONAL VARIATIONS

France is a diverse country, with each region offering its own unique landscape, climate, and way of life. Consequently, property prices and market conditions can vary significantly from one region to another. Popular areas, such as Paris and the French Riviera, tend to have higher property prices due to high demand, while more rural areas often offer more affordable options.

When considering where to buy a property in France, it's essential to research the regional variations and identify the specific areas that align with your preferences, budget, and long-term goals. Consider factors such as climate, local amenities, accessibility, and overall lifestyle when choosing your ideal region.

Property Types

The French real estate market offers a wide variety of property types to choose from, ranging from traditional stone farmhouses and half-timbered cottages to modern apartments and luxury villas. Some of the most common property types in France include:

• **Apartments (appartements):** Particularly common in urban areas, apartments can range from small studios to spacious multi-bedroom units, often located in historic buildings or modern complexes.

• **Houses (maisons):** Houses in France come in many styles, from traditional stone farmhouses and village cottages to contemporary villas and chalets. The style and size of houses can vary significantly depending on the region and local architectural traditions.

• **Chateaux and manor houses (châteaux et manoirs):** For those seeking a truly unique and luxurious property, France is home to numerous historic chateaux and manor houses, often set on expansive grounds and boasting stunning architectural features.

When searching for a property in France, consider the type of property that best suits your needs, lifestyle, and preferences. Be aware that different property types may come with different maintenance requirements, costs, and potential challenges, so it's essential to weigh these factors when making your decision.

Market Trends

As with any real estate market, the French property market is subject to fluctuations and trends. Factors such as economic conditions, political events, and demographic shifts can all impact the market and influence property prices and demand. It's important to stay informed about current market trends and to be prepared for potential changes in the market during your property search.

Some resources for tracking the French real estate market trends include:

• **National Institute for Statistical and Economic Studies (INSEE):** The INSEE publishes data on the French property market, including average property prices, sales volumes, and regional trends.

• **Notaires de France:** The French notary association provides regular reports and analysis on the real estate market, including regional and national statistics on property prices and sales.

• **Real estate agencies and property websites**: Many French real estate agencies and property websites publish articles and reports on the latest market trends and news, which can provide valuable insights into the current state of the market.

By staying informed about the French real estate market, you'll be better equipped to make informed decisions and navigate any potential challenges that may arise during your property search.

Understanding the French real estate market is a crucial first step in the process of buying a home in France. By familiarizing yourself with regional variations, property types, and market trends, you'll be better prepared to find the perfect property and successfully navigate the home buying process. Armed with this knowledge, you can approach the French property market with confidence and make well-informed decisions that will ultimately lead to a successful and rewarding property investment.

WORKING WITH REAL ESTATE AGENTS

One of the best ways to navigate the French real estate market is by working with a reputable real estate agent (agent immobilier). These professionals have in-depth knowledge of the local market and can help you find suitable properties, arrange viewings, and negotiate with sellers on your behalf. They can also provide valuable insights into local neighborhoods, amenities, and lifestyle factors that may influence your decision.

When choosing a real estate agent, it's essential to select someone with a strong track record and a solid understanding of the specific region in which you're interested. Look for agents who are members of professional organizations, such as the National Federation of French Real Estate Agents (FNAIM), as this indicates that they adhere to a strict code of ethics and professional standards.

Remember that real estate agents in France typically represent the seller, so it's important to keep this in mind when discussing your property search and negotiations. However, some agents specialize in working with buyers and can provide valuable assistance and guidance throughout the entire home buying process.

Legal Considerations

The process of buying a property in France involves several legal steps and requirements, which can be complex and unfamiliar to those new to the French property market. To ensure that your property purchase proceeds smoothly and without any legal complications, it's essential to be aware of the relevant laws and regulations and to seek professional assistance when necessary.

One of the most important legal professionals involved in the French property buying process is the notary (notaire). Notaries are government-appointed officials who oversee property transactions and ensure that all necessary taxes, fees, and paperwork are completed correctly. They also conduct searches on the property to ensure there are no outstanding debts, liens, or other legal issues that could impact the sale.

In addition to working with a notary, you may also wish to consult with a French property lawyer (avocat) who can provide specialized legal advice and assistance throughout the home buying process. This can be particularly useful for non-French speakers or those who are unfamiliar with the intricacies of French property law.

By understanding the legal aspects of the French real estate market and seeking professional assistance when necessary, you can minimize the risk of legal complications and ensure a smooth and successful property purchase.

Getting started in the French real estate market requires a solid understanding of regional variations, property types, market trends, and the roles of various professionals involved in the process. By familiarizing yourself with these aspects and seeking the guidance of experienced real estate agents, notaries, and lawyers, you can confidently navigate the French property market and make informed decisions that will ultimately lead to a successful and rewarding home purchase in France.

REGIONAL DIFFERENCES AND POPULAR LOCATIONS IN FRANCE

France is a diverse country, offering a wide array of landscapes, climates, and lifestyles across its many regions. Each region has its own distinct character, culture, and appeal, which can significantly influence the property market and the types of properties available. In this section, we'll explore some of the key regional differences and popular locations in France, providing an overview of what each region has to offer and the factors that may influence your property search.

1. Île-de-France

Paris

As the capital city and cultural heart of France, Paris is known for its iconic landmarks, world-class museums, and vibrant arts scene. The Parisian property market is highly competitive, with property prices significantly higher than in other regions of France. However, the city offers a unique and unparalleled living experience, with a diverse range of property types, from historic Haussmann-style apartments to contemporary penthouses.

Versailles

Located just a short distance from Paris, Versailles is known for its stunning palace and beautiful gardens, as well as its elegant architecture and charming historic center. Property prices in Versailles can be more affordable than in Paris, although still relatively high compared to other regions. The area is popular among families and professionals looking for a more relaxed lifestyle while remaining within easy commuting distance of the capital.

2. Provence-Alpes-Côte d'Azur

French Riviera

The French Riviera, also known as the Côte d'Azur, is a popular destination for property buyers seeking a luxurious and glamorous lifestyle, with its stunning coastline, warm climate, and glamorous towns such as Cannes, Nice, and Saint-Tropez. Property prices in the French Riviera can be quite high, particularly in the most sought-after locations, but the region offers a wide range of property types, from chic apartments to opulent villas.

Provence

Characterized by its picturesque landscapes, sun-soaked vineyards, and charming villages, Provence is a popular choice among those seeking a more traditional and tranquil French lifestyle. Property prices in Provence can vary significantly, with more affordable options available in rural areas and smaller villages. The region offers a variety of property styles, including traditional stone farmhouses, village houses, and country estates.

3. Occitanie

Toulouse

Known as the "Pink City" due to its distinctive red brick architecture, Toulouse is a vibrant and dynamic city with a thriving economy and a strong property market. Property prices in Toulouse are generally more affordable than in Paris or the French Riviera, making it an attractive option for those seeking a city lifestyle without the high price tag. The city offers a range of property types, including apartments, townhouses, and suburban homes.

Languedoc

Stretching from the Mediterranean coast to the Pyrenees mountains, Languedoc is a diverse and captivating region known for its beautiful landscapes, historic cities, and rich cultural heritage. Property prices in Languedoc can be quite affordable, particularly in rural areas and smaller towns. The region offers a wide range of property styles, from traditional village houses and stone farmhouses to modern villas and coastal apartments.

4. Nouvelle-Aquitaine

Bordeaux

Famous for its world-renowned wine production and elegant architecture, Bordeaux is a vibrant and sophisticated city that has experienced significant growth and regeneration in recent years. Property prices in Bordeaux are generally more affordable than in Paris, although the market has been steadily increasing. The city offers a range of property types, from historic apartments and townhouses to contemporary suburban homes.

Dordogne

Known for its picturesque landscapes, medieval villages, and prehistoric cave art, the Dordogne region in southwestern France is a popular destination for those seeking a rural and historic setting. Property prices in Dordogne are relatively affordable, particularly when compared to more urban locations or coastal areas. The region offers a variety of property styles, including traditional stone farmhouses, country estates, and charming village houses.

5. Brittany

Located in the northwest of France, Brittany is known for its rugged coastline, sandy beaches, and distinctive Celtic heritage. The region offers a mix of coastal and rural living, with a range of property types available, from traditional Breton cottages and longères to modern apartments and seaside villas. Property prices in Brittany can vary significantly depending on the location, with coastal areas often commanding higher prices than more inland locations.

6. Normandy

Famous for its historic D-Day landing beaches, picturesque countryside, and iconic Mont Saint-Michel, Normandy is a region steeped in history and natural beauty. The property market in Normandy offers a range of options for buyers, from traditional half-timbered houses and stone farmhouses to modern apartments and coastal properties. Property prices in Normandy can be quite reasonable, particularly in rural areas and smaller towns.

7. Loire Valley

Known as the "Garden of France," the Loire Valley is renowned for its stunning chateaux, lush vineyards, and charming villages. The region offers a diverse range of property types, from historic manor houses and chateaux to traditional village houses and modern apartments. Property prices in the Loire Valley can vary significantly depending on the location and property type, with more prestigious and historic properties commanding higher prices.

8. Auvergne-Rhône-Alpes

Lyon

As the third-largest city in France, Lyon is known for its rich history, vibrant culture, and thriving economy. The city offers a diverse range of property types, from historic apartments in the UNESCO-listed Old Town to modern family homes in the suburbs. Property prices in Lyon are generally more affordable than in Paris or other major cities, making it an attractive option for those seeking an urban lifestyle without the high price tag.

French Alps

The French Alps are a popular destination for property buyers seeking a mountain retreat or an investment in a ski resort. The region offers a wide range of property types, from cozy chalets and apartments to luxurious mountain estates. Property prices in the French Alps can vary significantly depending on the location and resort, with more prestigious and popular ski resorts commanding higher prices.

France's diverse regions offer a wide range of property types, landscapes, and lifestyles for prospective homebuyers to choose from. By understanding the regional differences and popular locations, you can identify the areas that best align with your preferences, budget, and long-term goals. With thorough research and careful consideration of the factors that may influence your property search, you'll be well on your way to finding your dream home in France.

□

TYPES OF PROPERTIES AVAILABLE IN FRANCE

France offers a diverse and enticing range of property types, from traditional farmhouses and village homes to modern apartments and luxury villas. Each property type has its own unique charm, features, and potential advantages or challenges, so it's important to carefully consider which type of property best suits your needs, preferences, and budget. In this section, we'll explore some of the most common property types available in France and discuss their characteristics and appeal.

1. Traditional Stone Farmhouses (Mas)

Traditional stone farmhouses, also known as "mas," are a quintessential feature of the French countryside, particularly in the southern regions of Provence and Languedoc. These charming properties often feature thick stone walls, exposed wooden beams, and terracotta tiled roofs, providing a rustic and authentic living experience.

Many traditional farmhouses have been lovingly restored and modernized, offering a unique blend of old-world charm and contemporary comforts. They often come with generous plots of land, making them ideal for those seeking a rural retreat, a smallholding, or even a vineyard. However, buyers should be prepared for the potential maintenance and renovation costs associated with older properties.

2. Village Houses (Maison de village)

Village houses are a popular property type in France, particularly in smaller towns and rural areas. These properties are typically built from local materials such as stone or brick and are often attached or semi-detached, offering a more compact living space than larger farmhouses or country estates.

One of the key appeals of village houses is their sense of community and the opportunity to immerse oneself in the local culture and way of life. Village houses often come with small gardens or courtyards, providing a private outdoor space. Buyers should be aware that these properties may have limited parking or require some renovation work, depending on their age and condition.

3. Half-Timbered Houses (Maison à colombages)

Half-timbered houses, known as "maison à colombages" in French, are characterized by their distinctive exposed timber framing and infill panels, often made from brick, plaster, or wattle and daub. This architectural style is particularly common in the northern regions of France, such as Normandy and Brittany, as well as in the Alsace region.

These historic and charming properties can offer a unique living experience, with many featuring original details such as fireplaces, wooden beams, and ornate carvings. As with other older properties, potential buyers should be prepared for the maintenance and renovation costs that may be associated with half-timbered houses.

4. Chateaux and Manor Houses (Châteaux et Manoirs)

For those seeking a truly unique and luxurious property, France is home to numerous historic chateaux and manor houses. These prestigious properties often boast stunning architectural features, expansive grounds, and a rich history, making them ideal for buyers seeking a one-of-a-kind investment or a grand family residence.

Chateaux and manor houses can vary significantly in size, style, and condition, with some requiring significant restoration or modernization. Buyers should be aware of the potential costs and challenges associated with maintaining and renovating these historic properties, as well as any legal restrictions or requirements related to their preservation.

5. Modern Villas

Modern villas are a popular property type in France, particularly in the coastal regions of the French Riviera and the Mediterranean. These contemporary properties often feature sleek architectural designs, high-quality finishes, and luxurious amenities such as swimming pools, landscaped gardens, and outdoor entertaining areas.

Modern villas can offer a low-maintenance and comfortable living experience, with many properties designed to take full advantage of their surrounding views and natural landscapes. However, buyers should be prepared for the potentially higher price tags and ongoing costs associated with these luxurious properties, as well as any potential restrictions related to local planning regulations or building codes.

6. Apartments (Appartements)

Apartments are a common property type in French cities, such as Paris, Lyon, and Marseille, as well as in popular tourist destinations and coastal areas. French apartments can range from compact studio spaces to spacious multi-bedroom units, offering a variety of options for buyers seeking an urban lifestyle or a low-maintenance holiday home.

One of the key advantages of apartment living is the convenience and access to amenities, such as shops, restaurants, public transportation, and cultural attractions. Buyers should be aware of the potential additional costs associated with apartment ownership, such as homeowners' association fees, service charges, and shared maintenance costs.

7. Ski Chalets

The French Alps and other mountainous regions of France are home to a wide range of ski chalets, offering the perfect retreat for winter sports enthusiasts and mountain lovers. Ski chalets can range from cozy, traditional wooden cabins to luxurious modern properties with high-end amenities and stunning mountain views.

Ski chalets can offer strong rental potential during the ski season, making them an attractive investment for those looking to generate rental income. However, buyers should consider the costs associated with maintaining a ski chalet, as well as any potential restrictions or requirements related to local planning regulations, building codes, or tourism development.

8. Lofts and Converted Spaces

In recent years, there has been growing interest in lofts and converted spaces in France, particularly in urban areas and former industrial regions. These unique properties often feature open-plan living spaces, high ceilings, and large windows, providing a contemporary and versatile living environment.

Converted spaces can include former factories, warehouses, or even historic buildings, offering a unique blend of character and modern style. Buyers should be aware that these properties may come with additional challenges or restrictions related to their conversion, renovation, or preservation, as well as potential issues related to noise, parking, or access to amenities.

The French property market offers a diverse and appealing range of property types for buyers to choose from, catering to a variety of lifestyles, preferences, and budgets. By understanding the unique features, advantages, and potential challenges associated with each property type, you can make an informed decision about which type of property best suits your needs and aspirations. With careful research and consideration, you'll be well on your way to finding the perfect French property to call home.

□

KEY FACTORS THAT INFLUENCE PROPERTY PRICES IN FRANCE

When purchasing a property in France, it is essential to understand the factors that can influence property prices. These factors can vary significantly depending on the region, location, and property type. By considering these factors and their potential impact on your property search, you can make informed decisions and maximize the value of your investment. In this section, we'll explore some of the key factors that can influence property prices in France.

1. Location

Location is one of the most critical factors that can impact property prices in France. Properties in desirable locations, such as popular tourist destinations, major cities, or sought-after coastal areas, tend to command higher prices than those in less popular or remote locations. Additionally, properties with desirable views, easy access to amenities, or close proximity to transportation networks can also demand higher prices.

When considering the location of a property, it's essential to evaluate factors such as the local economy, job market, and demand for rental properties, as these can also influence property prices and potential rental returns.

2. Property Type and Condition

The type and condition of a property can significantly affect its price, with certain property types, such as historic chateaux, modern villas, or luxury apartments, commanding higher prices than more modest or traditional property styles. Additionally, the condition of a property can play a significant role in determining its value, with well-maintained or recently renovated properties often demanding higher prices than those in need of significant repairs or modernization.

When evaluating a property, it's essential to consider factors such as the age, style, construction materials, and any unique features or architectural details, as these can all impact its value and potential appeal to buyers or renters.

3. Market Trends and Economic Factors

The overall state of the French property market and wider economy can also influence property prices. Factors such as interest rates, exchange rates, and inflation can all impact the affordability of property and the demand from both domestic and international buyers.

Furthermore, local market trends can play a significant role in shaping property prices. For example, in areas experiencing strong economic growth or an influx of new residents, property prices may be on the rise, while in areas with a stagnant economy or declining population, property prices may be more stable or even decreasing.

It's essential to stay informed about the latest market trends and economic indicators in your chosen area to ensure you're making informed decisions about your property purchase.

4. Supply and Demand

The balance between supply and demand can significantly influence property prices in France. In areas with a high demand for properties, such as popular tourist destinations or major cities, property prices may be driven up due to competition among buyers. Conversely, in areas with a surplus of properties or low demand, property prices may be more negotiable, as sellers may be more willing to accept lower offers in order to secure a sale.

When considering the supply and demand dynamics in your chosen area, it's essential to evaluate factors such as the local population growth, tourism industry, and property development trends, as these can all impact the availability and desirability of properties on the market.

5. Local Amenities and Infrastructure

The availability and quality of local amenities and infrastructure can also play a significant role in determining property prices in France. Properties located near schools, hospitals, shops, restaurants, and other essential amenities are often more desirable to buyers and renters, and may command higher prices as a result.

Similarly, properties with easy access to transportation networks, such as highways, train stations, or airports, can also be more appealing to buyers and renters, potentially leading to higher property prices. When evaluating a property's location, it's important to consider the availability and quality of local amenities and infrastructure, as these factors can significantly impact its value and long-term appeal.

6. Rental Potential and Investment Returns

For those looking to purchase a property in France as an investment or rental property, the potential rental income and investment returns can be significant factors in determining property prices. Properties with strong rental potential, such as those in popular tourist destinations or major cities, may command higher prices due to their ability to generate consistent rental income.

When evaluating the rental potential of a property, it's essential to consider factors such as the local rental market, seasonality, competition from other rental properties, and any legal restrictions or requirements related to short-term rentals. Additionally, it's crucial to factor in the costs associated with managing and maintaining a rental property, as these can also impact the overall return on investment.

7. Planning Regulations and Development Potential

Planning regulations and development potential can also influence property prices in France. Properties with the potential for expansion or development, such as those with large plots of land or existing planning permissions, may command higher prices due to their increased flexibility and future potential.

However, potential buyers should be aware of any local planning restrictions or requirements, as these can impact the feasibility of development projects or the potential return on investment. When considering a property with development potential, it's essential to consult with local planning authorities and conduct thorough research to ensure you're fully informed about any restrictions or requirements that may apply.

8. Historic and Cultural Factors

France is home to a rich cultural heritage and numerous historic properties, which can also impact property prices. Properties with historic significance, unique architectural features, or cultural importance may command higher prices due to their rarity and appeal to buyers seeking a one-of-a-kind property.

However, potential buyers should be aware of the potential costs and challenges associated with maintaining and renovating historic properties, as well as any legal restrictions or requirements related to their preservation. When considering a historic or culturally significant property, it's important to conduct thorough research and consult with local authorities and preservation organizations to ensure you're fully informed about any potential restrictions or requirements.

Understanding the key factors that influence property prices in France is essential to making informed decisions and maximizing the value of your investment. By carefully considering factors such as location, property type, market trends, supply and demand, local amenities, rental potential, planning regulations, and historic or cultural significance, you can identify the properties that best align with your needs, preferences, and budget. With thorough research and a clear understanding of the factors that can impact property prices, you'll be well-equipped to navigate the French property market and find your dream home or investment property.

□

FRENCH PROPERTY MARKET TRENDS AND FORECASTS

Understanding the latest trends and forecasts in the French property market is crucial for making informed decisions about buying a property in France. In this section, we will explore some of the key trends and forecasts that can help you better understand the current state of the market and its potential future trajectory. This knowledge will allow you to make strategic decisions about your property investment and stay ahead of the curve.

1. Post-COVID Recovery and Resilience

The COVID-19 pandemic has had a significant impact on property markets worldwide, including France. However, the French property market has demonstrated remarkable resilience and is expected to continue its recovery as vaccination rates increase, and life returns to a semblance of normalcy.

This resilience can be attributed to several factors, including low-interest rates, government support measures, and a strong desire among buyers for more spacious properties with outdoor spaces following lockdowns. As the economy recovers and restrictions ease, we can expect a continued uptick in demand for French properties, particularly in rural and suburban areas that offer a higher quality of life.

2. The Shift to Remote Work and Rural Properties

The pandemic has accelerated the shift towards remote work, with many companies adopting flexible work policies that allow employees to work from home, at least part-time. This trend has led to an increased interest in rural and suburban properties, as buyers seek out larger homes with more outdoor space and a better quality of life.

As remote work becomes more prevalent, we can expect this trend to continue, with growing demand for properties in more rural areas or smaller towns and villages. This shift in buyer preferences may also contribute to a rebalancing of property prices between urban and rural areas, as the demand for city-center properties decreases.

3. Low-Interest Rates and Affordable Financing

One of the key factors contributing to the current strength of the French property market is the historically low-interest rates, which have made financing a property purchase more affordable for many buyers. These low rates have helped to boost demand for French properties, particularly among first-time buyers and international investors.

While interest rates are expected to remain low for the foreseeable future, potential buyers should be aware that rates may rise eventually, which could impact the affordability of property financing. It's essential to carefully consider the potential implications of interest rate changes on your property investment and plan accordingly.

4. The Attraction of French Lifestyle and Culture

The French lifestyle and culture continue to be a major draw for international buyers, particularly those from the UK, other European countries, and the US. This enduring appeal is reflected in the steady demand for French properties, despite the challenges presented by the pandemic and other global events.

The French government has also made efforts to attract foreign buyers, such as offering favorable tax incentives and streamlining the process for obtaining residency permits. This focus on attracting international buyers is expected to continue, which bodes well for the future of the French property market.

5. The Impact of Brexit on British Buyers

Brexit has introduced new challenges for British buyers looking to purchase property in France, including changes to residency rules and potential tax implications. However, the appeal of French properties remains strong among British buyers, many of whom view France as a desirable destination for a second home or retirement property.

In the coming years, we can expect British buyers to continue to be a significant presence in the French property market, though the overall impact of Brexit on this demographic remains to be seen. British buyers will need to stay informed about the evolving post-Brexit regulations and requirements, and consider how these may impact their property search and investment plans.

6. The Rise of Environmentally Sustainable Properties

Environmental sustainability has become an increasingly important factor for many property buyers, with growing interest in eco-friendly homes and energy -efficient features. As awareness of climate change and the need for sustainable living grows, we can expect this trend to continue and even accelerate in the French property market.

Properties that incorporate eco-friendly features, such as solar panels, energy-efficient heating systems, or sustainable construction materials, are likely to become more attractive to buyers and may command higher prices as a result. Additionally, government incentives and initiatives to promote energy efficiency and sustainability in the housing sector may further encourage this trend.

7. The Growing Popularity of Co-Living and Co-Working Spaces

The rise of remote work and the sharing economy has contributed to a growing interest in co-living and co-working spaces in France, particularly in urban areas. These spaces offer a flexible and affordable alternative to traditional property ownership or rental arrangements, with shared amenities and a focus on community-building.

As the demand for flexible living and working arrangements increases, we can expect the popularity of co-living and co-working spaces to continue growing, potentially impacting the traditional property market in urban areas. Investors and developers should pay close attention to this trend and consider how it might influence their property investment strategies.

8. The Aging Population and the Demand for Accessible Housing

France, like many other countries, is experiencing a demographic shift towards an aging population, with a growing number of seniors and retirees. This trend is expected to increase the demand for accessible housing, designed to accommodate the needs of older residents, such as single-story homes or properties with ground-floor living spaces and accessible bathrooms.

Developers and investors should consider the potential opportunities presented by this demographic shift, as the demand for accessible and age-friendly housing is likely to continue growing in the coming years.

Whether you're a first-time buyer, experienced investor, or simply looking to purchase a dream home in France, staying informed about market trends and forecasts can help you make the most of your property search and maximize the value of your investment. As the French property market continues to evolve, adapt, and grow, there's never been a better time to explore the opportunities it has to offer.

II: FINANCIAL CONSIDERATIONS FOR BUYING A HOUSE IN FRANCE

When planning to purchase a property in France, it's crucial to carefully consider the various financial aspects involved. Understanding the costs, financing options, and tax implications can help you make informed decisions and budget appropriately for your investment. In this section, we'll outline some of the key financial considerations you should take into account when buying a house in France.

ESTIMATING YOUR BUDGET FOR BUYING A HOUSE IN FRANCE

When considering buying a house in France, one of the most crucial steps is to estimate your budget accurately. This will not only help you identify the properties that are within your financial reach but also assist in planning for the various costs involved in the purchase and ownership of a property. In this section, we'll guide you through the process of estimating your budget for buying a house in France, covering the essential aspects to consider.

1. Assess Your Financial Situation

Before you begin searching for a property in France, it's essential to take a close look at your current financial situation. This includes evaluating your income, savings, investments, and any outstanding debts. This assessment will help you determine how much you can comfortably afford to spend on a property without jeopardizing your financial stability.

• **Income**: Consider your current income sources, such as salary, rental income, dividends, or pensions. Be realistic about your future income prospects, taking into account factors such as job security, potential career progression, and the possibility of changes in your personal circumstances.

• **Savings and investments**: Determine the amount of money you have available in savings and investments that can be used towards your property purchase. This may include funds held in bank accounts, stocks, bonds, or other investments.

• **Outstanding debts:** Assess your current debt levels, including credit card balances, personal loans, and existing mortgages. It's essential to ensure that your debt-to-income ratio remains manageable and that you can comfortably service your existing debts while taking on the additional financial responsibility of a French property.

2. Determine Your Down Payment

The down payment is the amount of money you pay upfront towards the purchase of your property. In France, the typical down payment required for a mortgage is at least 20% of the property's purchase price. However, the more substantial the down payment you can make, the lower your monthly mortgage repayments will be and the less interest you'll pay over the loan term.

Consider the following factors when determining your down payment:

• **Your savings:** Assess the funds you have available for a down payment, taking into account the need to retain an emergency fund and maintain financial stability.

• **Gifts and financial support**: If you have family or friends willing to contribute towards your down payment, factor this into your calculations.

• **Equity release:** If you own a property in your home country, you may be able to release equity from that property to fund your down payment for a French property.

3. Calculate Your Borrowing Capacity

Once you have a clear understanding of your financial situation and down payment, the next step is to determine how much you can afford to borrow for your property purchase. Your borrowing capacity is primarily influenced by your income, outstanding debts, and credit history.

• **Debt-to-income ratio**: Lenders will typically look at your debt-to-income ratio when assessing your mortgage application. This ratio is calculated by dividing your total monthly debt payments by your gross monthly income. A lower debt-to-income ratio indicates a lower risk for the lender and may result in a higher borrowing capacity.

• **Credit history**: A good credit history is essential for securing a mortgage at a competitive interest rate. If you have a history of late payments, defaults, or other negative marks on your credit report, this may negatively impact your borrowing capacity.

• **Interest rates:** The interest rate on your mortgage will significantly affect your monthly repayments and the total amount you can afford to borrow. Shop around and compare mortgage offers from different lenders to find the best interest rate for your circumstances.

4. Estimate the Total Costs of Property Purchase

As previously mentioned, there are several costs associated with buying a house in France, beyond the property's purchase price.

When estimating your budget, it's essential to account for these additional costs, which include:

• **Notary fees:** These fees, which typically range from 7% to 10% of the property price, cover registration taxes, stamp duty, and legal fees for the notary handling the transaction.

• **Estate agent fees:** If you use an estate agent to assist with your property search and purchase, you will need to pay their fees, which can range from 3% to 10% of the property price.

• **Mortgage arrangement fees:** If you require a mortgage to finance your property purchase, you may need to pay arrangement fees to the lender, which can vary depending on the mortgage product and lender.

• **Survey and inspection fees:** It's recommended to have a property survey and inspection carried out before purchasing a property in France. The cost of these services can vary depending on the property size and location.

Ensure you factor these costs into your budget, as they can significantly impact the overall affordability of your property purchase.

5. Plan for Ongoing Costs

In addition to the upfront costs of purchasing a property in France, you should also budget for ongoing costs associated with property ownership. These costs can include:

• **Property taxes:** In France, property owners are typically responsible for the taxe foncière, while occupants (owners or tenants) pay the taxe d'habitation. These taxes can vary depending on the property's location and size.

• **Maintenance and repairs:** Regular maintenance is essential to keep your property in good condition, and you'll need to budget for any necessary repairs or improvements.

• **Utilities**: You'll be responsible for the costs of utilities such as electricity, water, and gas, as well as any service charges for communal facilities if your property is part of a larger development.

• **Insurance**: Ensure you research and budget for building, contents, and liability insurance premiums to protect your property and belongings.

• **Management fees:** If you plan to rent out your property, you may need to pay management fees to a property management company or rental agency to handle tasks such as tenant vetting, rent collection, and property maintenance.

6. Consider Potential Rental Income

If you plan to rent out your French property, either as a holiday rental or a long-term rental, you should factor the potential rental income into your budget calculations. Rental income can help offset the costs of property ownership and contribute to your mortgage repayments.

However, it's essential to be realistic about the rental potential of your property. Research the local rental market, considering factors such as average rental prices, occupancy rates, and seasonal variations. Additionally, account for any costs associated with renting out your property, such as management fees, cleaning and maintenance, and taxes on rental income.

By carefully estimating your budget and considering all the financial aspects involved in purchasing a house in France, you'll be well-prepared to make informed decisions about your property investment. A thorough understanding of your financial situation, borrowing capacity, and the various costs associated with property ownership will enable you to confidently navigate the French property market and find a property that meets your needs and budget.

□

UNDERSTANDING THE COSTS OF BUYING A HOUSE IN FRANCE

When buying a house in France, it's crucial to have a clear understanding of the various costs associated with property acquisition and ownership. In this section, we'll break down the main expenses you'll need to consider when budgeting for your French property purchase, helping you make informed decisions and avoid any financial surprises along the way.

1. Property Purchase Price

The most obvious cost when buying a house in France is the property's purchase price. Property prices can vary significantly depending on factors such as the property's location, size, age, and condition. When searching for a property, it's essential to have a clear understanding of your budget and be realistic about what you can afford.

2. Notary Fees

In France, property transactions are overseen by a notaire, a public official responsible for ensuring the legality of the sale and registering the property in the buyer's name. Notary fees typically range from 7% to 10% of the property's purchase price and include registration taxes, stamp duty, and the notary's legal fees. These fees are generally paid by the buyer at the time of the property purchase.

3. Estate Agent Fees

If you use an estate agent to help you find and purchase a property in France, you'll need to pay their fees. Estate agent fees in France can vary, but they typically range from 3% to 10% of the property's purchase price. In some cases, the fees may be shared between the buyer and the seller, while in other instances, the buyer may be responsible for the entire amount.

4. Mortgage Arrangement Fees

If you require a mortgage to finance your property purchase in France, you may need to pay arrangement fees to the lender. These fees cover the lender's administrative costs and can vary depending on the mortgage product and lender. In some cases, the arrangement fees may be added to the mortgage amount and repaid over the life of the loan.

5. Survey and Inspection Fees

Before purchasing a property in France, it's recommended to have a property survey and inspection carried out. This can help identify any potential issues with the property, such as structural defects, damp, or other problems that could result in costly repairs down the line. The cost of a survey and inspection can vary depending on the property's size, age, and location, but it's a worthwhile investment to protect yourself from potential issues.

6. Property Taxes

As a property owner in France, you'll be responsible for paying property taxes. There are two main property taxes in France:

- **Taxe foncière:** This tax is paid by the property owner and is based on the property's size, location, and other factors. The taxe foncière varies from one municipality to another, but you can generally expect to pay between 0.5% and 1.5% of the property's estimated rental value per year.

• **Taxe d'habitation**: This tax is paid by the property's occupant, whether they are the owner or a tenant. Like the taxe foncière, the taxe d'habitation is calculated based on the property's size, location, and other factors and can vary between municipalities. As a property owner, you'll need to factor this tax into your budget if you plan to live in the property or rent it out on a long-term basis.

7. Insurance

When purchasing a property in France, you'll need to arrange appropriate insurance coverage. This typically includes:

• **Building insurance**: This covers the structure of the property and any permanent fixtures and fittings, protecting you against damage caused by events such as fire, flood, or storm.

• **Contents insurance:** This covers your personal belongings and any furniture or appliances within the property, protecting you against loss or damage due to theft, fire, or other events.

• **Liability insurance:** This protects you against any claims for personal injury or property damage that may occur on your property. This type of insurance is particularly important if you plan to rent out your property, as it can provide coverage for any accidents or incidents involving your tenants.

The cost of insurance will depend on factors such as the property's location, size, and age, as well as the level of coverage you require. It's essential to shop around and compare insurance quotes to ensure you're getting the best deal.

8. Maintenance and Repairs

Owning a property in France comes with ongoing maintenance and repair costs. These can include routine maintenance, such as painting and decorating, as well as more significant repairs, such as fixing a leaky roof or replacing a broken boiler. It's essential to budget for these costs and set aside funds for any unexpected repairs that may arise.

9. Utilities

As a property owner in France, you'll be responsible for the costs of utilities such as electricity, water, and gas. The cost of utilities can vary depending on the property's size, location, and usage. Additionally, if your property is part of a larger development or apartment building, you may also need to pay service charges for communal facilities such as lifts, gardens, or swimming pools.

10. Property Management Fees

If you plan to rent out your French property, either as a holiday rental or a long-term rental, you may need to pay property management fees. These fees cover the cost of services such as tenant vetting, rent collection, and property maintenance and can vary depending on the property management company or rental agency you choose to work with.

11. Legal and Professional Fees

When buying a house in France, you may need to consult with legal and financial professionals to ensure you understand the various regulations, taxes, and financial implications associated with property ownership. These fees can include the cost of hiring a lawyer, accountant, or financial advisor and can vary depending on the professionals you choose to work with and the level of support you require.

Understanding the costs involved in buying a house in France is crucial to help you budget effectively and make informed decisions about your property purchase. By taking into account the various expenses associated with property acquisition and ownership, you can better assess the overall affordability of your property investment and plan for a smooth and successful property purchase in France.

MORTGAGE OPTIONS FOR FOREIGNERS

If you're a foreigner looking to buy a property in France, securing a mortgage can be a key factor in making your dream a reality. While obtaining a mortgage as a non-resident may present some challenges, it's certainly possible with the right preparation and research. In this section, we'll discuss the various mortgage options available to foreigners and provide guidance on how to navigate the French mortgage market.

1. French Banks and Mortgage Lenders

Many French banks and mortgage lenders are open to providing mortgages to non-residents, though they may have stricter eligibility criteria and require higher deposit amounts compared to French nationals. Some of the major French banks that offer mortgage products to non-residents include BNP Paribas, Crédit Agricole, Société Générale, and Banque Populaire.

When approaching a French bank or mortgage lender, it's essential to present a strong financial profile, including a stable income, good credit history, and sufficient savings to cover the required deposit and associated fees. You'll also need to provide various financial documents to support your mortgage application, such as payslips, bank statements, and tax returns.

2. International Banks and Mortgage Lenders

Some international banks and mortgage lenders also offer mortgage products specifically tailored to foreigners purchasing property in France. These lenders may have a better understanding of the unique challenges faced by non-residents and may be more flexible in their eligibility criteria.

When considering an international lender, it's essential to research their reputation, interest rates, and terms and conditions. Some well-known international banks that offer mortgages for French property purchases include Barclays, HSBC, and Lloyds Bank.

3. Mortgage Brokers

Working with a mortgage broker can be particularly beneficial for foreigners looking to secure a mortgage in France. Mortgage brokers have extensive knowledge of the French mortgage market and can help you identify the best mortgage products and lenders based on your individual circumstances.

A good mortgage broker will assess your financial profile, help you prepare the necessary documentation, and negotiate with lenders on your behalf. They can also provide valuable guidance on the French mortgage process and help you avoid potential pitfalls. While using a mortgage broker will incur additional fees, their expertise and support can be invaluable in securing a suitable mortgage.

4. Mortgage Types Available to Foreigners

When securing a mortgage in France, you'll need to consider the various mortgage types available and choose the one that best suits your needs and financial circumstances. Some of the most common mortgage types available to foreigners in France include:

• **Fixed-rate mortgages**: With a fixed-rate mortgage, the interest rate remains constant throughout the mortgage term. This offers stability and predictability, as your monthly repayments will not change during the fixed-rate period.

• **Variable-rate mortgages**: With a variable-rate mortgage, the interest rate can fluctuate based on changes in the market or the lender's standard variable rate. This can result in lower monthly repayments if interest rates decrease but can also lead to higher repayments if rates increase.

• **Interest-only mortgages**: With an interest-only mortgage, you only pay the interest on the loan each month, with the principal amount remaining unchanged. At the end of the mortgage term, you'll need to repay the entire principal amount, either through savings, investments, or the sale of the property. While this can result in lower monthly repayments, it does require careful financial planning to ensure you can repay the principal at the end of the term.

5. Loan-to-Value Ratios for Foreigners

When assessing your mortgage application, lenders will consider the loan-to-value (LTV) ratio, which is the amount you wish to borrow as a percentage of the property's value. In general, French banks and mortgage lenders require a lower LTV ratio for foreigners compared to French nationals. As a foreign buyer, you can generally expect to secure a mortgage with an LTV ratio of 60% to 85%. This means you'll need to provide a deposit of at least 15% to 40% of the property's value, depending on the lender's requirements.

6. Mortgage Term Lengths and Age Limits

Mortgage term lengths in France typically range from 10 to 25 years, with some lenders offering terms of up to 30 years. It's essential to consider the term length when selecting a mortgage, as it will impact your monthly repayments and the total amount of interest paid over the life of the loan.

In addition to term lengths, French banks and mortgage lenders also have age limits for borrowers. The maximum age at which a mortgage can be granted is generally between 70 and 75 years, depending on the lender's policies. This means that if you're an older borrower, you may need to opt for a shorter mortgage term or consider alternative financing options.

7. Mortgage Application Process

The mortgage application process in France can be complex, especially for foreigners who may be unfamiliar with French regulations and documentation requirements. To help ensure a smooth application process, it's essential to:

• Prepare all required financial documents, such as payslips, bank statements, and tax returns, and ensure they are translated into French if necessary.

• Obtain an "agreement in principle" from a lender, which is a preliminary approval based on your financial profile and documentation. This can help strengthen your position when negotiating property prices with sellers.

• Work closely with your mortgage broker or lender to ensure you understand the various steps involved in the application process and any deadlines that need to be met.

8. Mortgage Fees and Charges

When securing a mortgage in France, you'll need to budget for various fees and charges, including:

• **Mortgage arrangement fees**: These fees cover the lender's administrative costs and typically range from 1% to 1.5% of the mortgage amount.

• **Mortgage broker fees:** If you use a mortgage broker, you'll need to pay their fees, which can range from 1% to 3% of the mortgage amount.

• **Valuation fees**: Before approving your mortgage, the lender will require a property valuation to assess the property's value and ensure it's suitable security for the loan. Valuation fees can vary depending on the property's size, location, and value.

• **Early repayment charges**: If you choose to repay your mortgage early, either in part or in full, you may be subject to early repayment charges. These charges can vary depending on the lender and the mortgage product.

Obtaining a mortgage as a foreigner buying a house in France is achievable with the right preparation and research. By understanding the various mortgage options available, working with professionals such as mortgage brokers and lenders, and being aware of the associated fees and charges, you can secure a mortgage that meets your needs and financial circumstances, allowing you to realize your dream of owning a French property.

□

TAX IMPLICATIONS OF OWNING A PROPERTY IN FRANCE

Owning a property in France comes with various tax implications that can impact your overall financial planning and decision-making. It's essential to understand the French tax system and the various taxes associated with property ownership to avoid any unpleasant surprises and ensure you're prepared for your financial obligations. In this section, we'll discuss the main tax considerations for owning a property in France.

1. Wealth Tax (Impôt sur la Fortune Immobilière - IFI)

Wealth tax, known as Impôt sur la Fortune Immobilière (IFI), is a tax imposed on the net value of real estate assets owned by individuals in France. As of January 1, 2018, the IFI replaced the previous Impôt de Solidarité sur la Fortune (ISF), which was a tax on the overall wealth of individuals.

IFI applies to both residents and non-residents who own real estate in France, with the taxable value being determined based on the net value of the property (market value minus any outstanding loans). The tax is applicable if the net value of your real estate assets in France exceeds €1,300,000. The tax rates are progressive and range from 0.5% to 1.5% of the property value.

It's important to note that certain exemptions and reductions may apply, such as for properties used as a primary residence, agricultural land, or forestry holdings. Be sure to consult a tax advisor or specialist to understand your specific tax obligations.

2. Property Tax (Taxe Foncière)

Property tax, or Taxe Foncière, is an annual tax imposed on property owners in France. The tax is calculated based on the cadastral rental value of the property, which is an assessed value determined by the local authorities. The tax rate varies depending on the location of the property and the local tax rates set by the commune, department, and region.

Taxe Foncière is payable by the property owner, regardless of whether the property is occupied, rented out, or vacant. In some cases, if the property is rented out, the owner may pass the cost of the tax onto the tenant through the rental agreement.

3. Residence Tax (Taxe d'Habitation)

Residence tax, or Taxe d'Habitation, is an annual tax levied on the occupant of a property in France, whether they are the owner, tenant, or occupier. The tax is calculated based on the cadastral rental value of the property and the local tax rates set by the commune, department, and region.

However, significant changes to the Taxe d'Habitation have been introduced in recent years, with the tax being gradually phased out for the majority of French households. As of 2023, the Taxe d'Habitation has been completely abolished for primary residences. Nevertheless, the tax still applies to second homes and holiday homes, with the rates and exemptions varying depending on the property's location.

4. Capital Gains Tax (Impôt sur les Plus-Values)

When selling a property in France, you may be subject to capital gains tax (Impôt sur les Plus-Values) if you make a profit from the sale. The tax is calculated based on the difference between the property's purchase and sale price, taking into account certain allowable costs and expenses, such as acquisition costs, improvement works, and selling costs.

Capital gains tax rates in France differ for residents and non-residents. For French residents, the tax rate is 19% plus additional social charges, resulting in a total rate of 30.1%. For non-residents from EU countries, the rate is 19%, while non-residents from non-EU countries may be subject to a higher rate of 33.33%, depending on the tax treaty between France and their country of residence.

There are various exemptions and allowances that can reduce or eliminate your capital gains tax liability. For example, gains from the sale of your primary residence are exempt from capital gains tax. Additionally, there is a taper relief system in place, with the taxable gain reduced depending on the length of property ownership. After 22 years of ownership, the gain is exempt from the capital gains tax, and after 30 years, it is exempt from social charges as well.

5. Rental Income Tax

If you rent out your French property, you'll need to declare your rental income and pay taxes on it. The taxation of rental income depends on whether you're a resident or non-resident and the type of rental activity (furnished or unfurnished).

For French residents, rental income is taxed as part of their overall income, subject to the progressive French income tax rates. Social charges are also applicable at a rate of 17.2%.

Non-residents are subject to a withholding tax on their rental income, with the rate depending on their country of residence. For EU residents, the rate is 20%, while non-EU residents may be subject to a higher rate, depending on the tax treaty between France and their country of residence. It's essential to consult a tax advisor to understand your specific tax obligations as a non-resident landlord.

6. Inheritance Tax and Gift Tax

Inheritance tax and gift tax in France are levied on the transfer of assets, including property, following the death of the owner or as a gift during their lifetime. Both taxes apply to property located in France, regardless of the beneficiary's residency status.

Inheritance tax rates in France are progressive and depend on the relationship between the deceased or donor and the beneficiary. Spouses and civil partners are exempt from inheritance tax, while other beneficiaries may benefit from certain tax allowances, depending on their relationship with the deceased or donor.

Gift tax rates and allowances are similar to those of inheritance tax, with exemptions and allowances varying based on the relationship between the donor and the beneficiary.

It's essential to seek professional advice on estate planning and potential tax implications when owning a property in France, particularly for cross-border situations where the laws of multiple countries may apply.

By familiarizing yourself with the various taxes associated with property ownership, such as wealth tax, property tax, capital gains tax, rental income tax, and inheritance tax, you can ensure you're well-prepared to navigate the French tax system and enjoy your dream property in France.

□

CURRENCY EXCHANGE AND INTERNATIONAL TRANSACTIONS

When purchasing a property in France, it's highly likely that you'll need to exchange currency and make international transactions, particularly if you're a foreign buyer. Understanding how currency exchange and international transactions work is essential to ensure you're getting the best possible exchange rates, minimizing transaction costs, and efficiently managing your finances across borders. In this section, we'll discuss the key aspects of currency exchange and international transactions when buying a house in France.

1. Exchange Rate Fluctuations

Currency exchange rates are constantly fluctuating due to various factors, such as market demand, geopolitical events, and economic indicators. These fluctuations can have a significant impact on the cost of purchasing a property in France if you're converting funds from a different currency.

It's essential to monitor exchange rate movements and understand the factors that can affect currency values to make informed decisions about when to exchange your funds. By timing your currency exchange strategically, you can potentially save thousands on your property purchase.

2. Using a Currency Exchange Specialist

While it may seem convenient to use your bank for currency exchange and international transactions, banks often charge high fees and offer less competitive exchange rates compared to specialized currency exchange providers.

Currency exchange specialists, also known as foreign exchange (forex) brokers, focus solely on currency transactions and typically offer better exchange rates and lower fees than traditional banks. They can also provide personalized services, such as dedicated account managers, to help you navigate the currency exchange process and manage your international transactions.

When choosing a currency exchange specialist, be sure to:

• Check their regulatory status to ensure they're a licensed and reputable provider.

• Compare exchange rates and fees across multiple providers to find the best deal.

• Look for providers with a strong track record and positive customer reviews.

3. Forward Contracts and Currency Options

One way to protect yourself from exchange rate fluctuations when buying a property in France is to use a forward contract. A forward contract is an agreement between you and a currency exchange specialist to exchange a specific amount of currency at a predetermined exchange rate on a future date. This allows you to lock in the current exchange rate and avoid potential losses due to unfavorable exchange rate movements.

Another option to manage currency risk is to use currency options, which give you the right, but not the obligation, to exchange currency at a predetermined rate on a future date. This can be useful if you're uncertain about the timing of your property purchase but want to protect yourself against adverse exchange rate movements.

Both forward contracts and currency options can provide a level of certainty and protection for your international transactions, helping you manage your finances more effectively when buying a house in France.

4. Opening a French Bank Account

When purchasing a property in France, it's often necessary to open a French bank account to manage your finances locally. Having a French bank account can make it easier to pay for property-related expenses, such as taxes, utility bills, and maintenance costs, as well as receive rental income if you choose to rent out your property.

To open a French bank account, you'll need to provide various documents, such as proof of identity, proof of address, and proof of income. Banks may also require additional documents depending on your residency status and financial profile.

It's essential to research the various banking options available in France, as different banks may offer different account types, services, and fees. Some banks also provide specialized services for non-residents and expatriates, which can be beneficial if you're a foreign buyer.

5. International Money Transfers

When transferring funds internationally for your property purchase, it's important to understand the various fees and charges that may apply, such as:

• **Transfer fees**: These are fees charged by your bank or currency exchange specialist for processing the international money transfer. Transfer fees can vary widely between providers, so it's crucial to compare different options to find the most cost-effective solution.

• **Intermediary bank fees**: Sometimes, when sending money internationally, intermediary banks are involved in the transaction process. These banks may charge additional fees, which can increase the overall cost of your money transfer. To minimize intermediary bank fees, try to choose a provider that offers direct transfers or has partnerships with banks in both the sending and receiving countries.

• **Receiving bank fees**: The receiving bank, in this case, a French bank, may also charge fees for processing incoming international transfers. It's essential to understand these fees and factor them into your overall transaction costs.

• **Currency conversion fees:** When exchanging currency, banks and currency exchange specialists typically add a margin to the exchange rate they offer. This margin, known as the "spread," is the difference between the wholesale exchange rate (the rate at which banks and financial institutions trade currencies) and the rate offered to customers. To get the best exchange rate, compare the rates offered by different providers and consider using a currency exchange specialist that offers competitive rates and low fees.

6. Tax Implications of International Transactions

International transactions, such as transferring funds to France for your property purchase or repatriating rental income to your home country, may have tax implications. Depending on your country of residence and the specific transaction, you may be subject to taxes, such as capital gains tax, income tax, or withholding tax.

It's essential to consult a tax advisor or specialist familiar with both your home country's tax system and the French tax system to understand your specific tax obligations and ensure compliance with all relevant regulations.

7. Currency Exchange Risk Management Strategies

Given the potential impact of exchange rate fluctuations on your property purchase, it's crucial to have a currency risk management strategy in place. Some strategies to consider include:

• **Regularly monitoring exchange rates**: Keeping an eye on exchange rate movements can help you identify trends and make informed decisions about when to exchange your funds.

• **Using currency hedging tools**: As discussed earlier, forward contracts and currency options can provide a level of protection against adverse exchange rate movements, allowing you to manage your currency risk more effectively.

• **Diversifying your currency exposure**: If you have multiple sources of income or assets in different currencies, consider diversifying your currency exposure to minimize the impact of exchange rate fluctuations on your overall financial position.

By closely monitoring exchange rates, using a currency exchange specialist, employing currency hedging tools, and managing your finances effectively, you can save money on your property purchase and ensure a smooth experience throughout the entire process.

□

III: LEGAL FRAMEWORK

The legal framework in France plays a crucial role in the property buying process. French property law is based on a civil law system that emphasizes written regulations, contractual agreements, and the role of notaries. Key aspects include the property registration system, which ensures clear title and ownership rights, and the involvement of a notary, who acts as an impartial legal expert to oversee the transaction. It's essential to understand the legal requirements, such as the mandatory diagnostic reports and the cooling-off period, to ensure a smooth and successful property purchase. Engaging a French property lawyer or legal advisor can provide valuable guidance and support throughout the process.

OVERVIEW OF THE FRENCH LEGAL SYSTEM FOR PROPERTY OWNERSHIP

When buying a property in France, understanding the legal system and the specific regulations related to property ownership is essential to ensure a successful and hassle-free transaction. The French legal system for property ownership is based on a civil law system, which has several distinctive features compared to common law systems. In this section, we will provide an overview of the French legal system for property ownership and the key aspects you need to be aware of when purchasing a property in France.

1. Civil Law System

Unlike common law systems, where case law and judicial precedent play a significant role in shaping the law, the French legal system is based on a civil law system that emphasizes written regulations and codes. These codes, such as the French Civil Code, govern various aspects of property ownership, including property rights, inheritance rules, and contractual obligations. As a buyer, you should familiarize yourself with the relevant legal provisions to understand your rights and obligations in the property buying process.

2. The Role of Notaries

Notaries (notaires) play a critical role in the French property buying process, acting as impartial legal experts responsible for overseeing the transaction, verifying the legality of the property transfer, and ensuring the proper registration of property rights. Notaries are public officials, appointed by the Ministry of Justice, and are required to hold a specialized legal degree.

When buying a property in France, you will need to engage the services of a notary, who will be responsible for preparing the sale and purchase agreement (compromis de vente), conducting due diligence checks on the property, and preparing the final deed of sale (acte de vente). The notary's fees are typically paid by the buyer and are regulated by the French government.

3. Property Registration System

France has a well-established property registration system, which ensures clear title and ownership rights. When you purchase a property in France, the notary will register the property transfer with the local land registry (service de la publicité foncière), which records all property transactions and ownership rights.

This registration process ensures that any potential legal issues or disputes regarding the property are resolved before the transfer of ownership takes place. It also guarantees the buyer's rights as the new owner of the property, protecting them from any potential claims from third parties.

4. Mandatory Diagnostic Reports

When selling a property in France, the seller is legally required to provide a series of diagnostic reports, known as the Dossier de Diagnostic Technique (DDT). These reports cover various aspects of the property's condition, such as energy performance, asbestos, lead, termites, electrical and gas installations, and natural and technological risks.

As a buyer, you should carefully review these diagnostic reports to understand the property's condition and any potential issues that may require attention or remediation.

Failure to provide these reports can result in penalties for the seller and may also give the buyer grounds to renegotiate the purchase price or terminate the contract.

5. Cooling-off Period

After signing the compromis de vente, the buyer has a 10-day cooling-off period, during which they have the right to withdraw from the purchase without any penalty or obligation. This cooling-off period is intended to provide buyers with time to reflect on their decision and seek any necessary legal, financial, or property advice before committing to the purchase.

If the buyer decides to withdraw from the purchase during the cooling-off period, they must notify the seller in writing, either by registered mail, email, or hand delivery, before the end of the 10-day period.

Understanding the French legal system for property ownership is essential when buying a house in France. By familiarizing yourself with the key aspects of the legal process, such as the role of notaries, the property registration system, mandatory diagnostic reports, and the cooling-off period, you can ensure a smooth and successful property purchase. It's advisable to engage a French property lawyer or legal advisor to guide you through the process and help you navigate the complexities of the French legal system, safeguarding your interests and protecting your investment.

TYPES OF PROPERTY OWNERSHIP IN FRANCE

When buying a property in France, it's essential to understand the different types of property ownership available and their implications. Each ownership type has its unique set of rules, rights, and obligations, which can affect various aspects of your property purchase, such as taxation, inheritance, and property management. In this section, we'll explore the main types of property ownership in France, including full ownership, shared ownership, leaseback properties, and co-ownership.

1. Full Ownership (Pleine Propriété)

Full ownership, or "pleine propriété" in French, is the most common and straightforward form of property ownership in France. When you purchase a property under full ownership, you have complete and exclusive rights to the property, including the land on which it stands, and any associated buildings or structures.

As the full owner of the property, you have the right to:

• Use the property as you see fit, within the bounds of local planning regulations and building codes.

• Sell or lease the property, without any restrictions or limitations.

• Make improvements or modifications to the property, subject to obtaining any necessary permits or approvals.

Full ownership also comes with various responsibilities and obligations, such as:

• Paying property taxes, including the taxe foncière (land tax) and taxe d'habitation (residential tax) if the property is your primary residence.

• Maintaining and managing the property in accordance with local regulations.

• Complying with French inheritance laws, which may affect your ability to dispose of the property upon your death.

2. Shared Ownership (Indivision)

Shared ownership, known as "indivision" in French, occurs when two or more individuals jointly own a property. Each owner, or "co-indivisaire," holds a share of the property, which can be equal or unequal depending on the terms of the ownership agreement.

Under shared ownership, each co-owner has the right to use and enjoy the property, but decisions regarding the property's management, maintenance, or sale must be made jointly and agreed upon by all co-owners. In some cases, disagreements or disputes among co-owners can lead to difficulties in managing the property or making important decisions.

To avoid potential conflicts, it's advisable to have a shared ownership agreement in place, which sets out the rights and responsibilities of each co-owner, as well as procedures for resolving disputes and making decisions regarding the property. This agreement can be drafted by a notary and registered with the local land registry.

3. Leaseback Properties (Loueur en Meublé Non Professionnel)

Leaseback properties, or "loueur en meublé non professionnel" (LMNP) in French, are a unique type of property ownership that combines elements of full ownership and leasing. Under this arrangement, you purchase a property within a managed development, such as a holiday resort, and then lease it back to a management company for a specified period (usually between 9 and 20 years).

The management company is responsible for maintaining the property, renting it out to tourists or other short-term tenants, and paying you a guaranteed rental income during the leaseback period. At the end of the leaseback period, you regain full ownership of the property and can choose to continue renting it out, use it yourself, or sell it.

Leaseback properties can be an attractive investment option for those looking for a hands-off approach to property ownership and a source of rental income. However, it's essential to carefully review the terms of the leaseback agreement and understand the potential risks and limitations, such as restrictions on personal use of the property and the dependence on the management company's performance.

4. Co-ownership (Copropriété)

Co-ownership, or "copropriété" in French, is a form of property ownership commonly found in apartment buildings and multi-unit developments. Under co-ownership, you own a private unit within the development, as well as a share of the common areas and facilities, such as the building's entrance, staircase, gardens, and any shared amenities like swimming pools or gyms.

In a co-ownership arrangement, the management and maintenance of the common areas are overseen by a co-ownership association, known as the "syndicat des copropriétaires." Each co-owner is a member of this association and has the right to participate in decision-making processes through regular meetings, known as general assemblies.

Co-owners are also responsible for contributing to the costs of maintaining and managing the common areas, typically through monthly or annual charges, known as "charges de copropriété." These charges are calculated based on each co-owner's share of the common areas, which is determined by the size and value of their private unit.

When buying a property under co-ownership, it's essential to understand your rights and responsibilities as a co-owner, as well as any rules or regulations governing the use and management of the common areas. It's also crucial to review the financial health of the co-ownership association and any potential liabilities or upcoming expenses, such as major repairs or renovations, which could impact your charges de copropriété.

5. Tontine Clause

In addition to the above types of property ownership, it's worth mentioning the tontine clause, which can be included in the property purchase agreement for shared ownership or co-ownership situations. The tontine clause stipulates that, upon the death of one of the co-owners, their share of the property automatically transfers to the surviving co-owner(s), bypassing French inheritance laws and any potential inheritance tax liabilities.

The tontine clause can be useful for unmarried couples or non-traditional family structures, who may not be subject to the same inheritance rights and protections as married couples or direct family members. However, it's important to note that the tontine clause can have complex legal and tax implications and should only be used after careful consideration and consultation with a French property lawyer or legal advisor.

Each ownership type has its unique set of rules, rights, and obligations, which can affect different aspects of your property purchase and ownership experience. By familiarizing yourself with the different ownership types and consulting with a French property lawyer or legal advisor, you can make an informed decision about the best ownership structure for your needs and ensure a successful property purchase.

THE ROLE OF THE NOTAIRE IN PROPERTY TRANSACTIONS

In France, the notaire plays a crucial role in property transactions, ensuring that all legal requirements are met and the transfer of property ownership proceeds smoothly. Notaires are public officials appointed by the Ministry of Justice, who have a legal duty to provide impartial advice and act in the best interests of all parties involved in a property transaction. In this section, we will explore the role of the notaire in property transactions, outlining their responsibilities and the various stages of the property buying process in which they are involved.

1. Preparing the Sale and Purchase Agreement

The first key responsibility of the notaire in a property transaction is to prepare the sale and purchase agreement, known as the "compromis de vente" or "promesse de vente." This document outlines the terms and conditions of the property sale, including the agreed-upon purchase price, the completion date, and any special conditions or contingencies that must be met before the transaction can proceed.

The notaire will ensure that the sale and purchase agreement accurately reflects the intentions of both the buyer and the seller, as well as complies with French property law and regulations. They will also verify the legal status of the property and the seller's right to sell, conducting necessary searches in the land registry and checking for any potential issues or disputes related to the property.

2. Conducting Due Diligence

Once the sale and purchase agreement is signed, the notaire is responsible for conducting due diligence on the property. This process involves verifying the property's legal status, title, and ownership rights, as well as ensuring that all required diagnostic reports have been provided by the seller.

The notaire will also check for any outstanding mortgages or liens on the property, which must be cleared before the transfer of ownership can take place. They will liaise with the local land registry to confirm the property's boundaries, zoning regulations, and any easements or rights of way that may affect the property.

3. Preparing the Final Deed of Sale

Upon completion of the due diligence process and the fulfillment of any special conditions or contingencies outlined in the sale and purchase agreement, the notaire will prepare the final deed of sale, known as the "acte de vente" or "acte authentique." This document formalizes the transfer of property ownership from the seller to the buyer and is legally binding upon both parties.

The notaire will ensure that the final deed of sale accurately reflects the terms of the sale and purchase agreement, as well as complies with all relevant French property laws and regulations. They will also calculate and collect any taxes and fees associated with the property transaction, such as the registration fees and notaire's fees, which are typically paid by the buyer.

4. Registering the Property Transfer

After the signing of the final deed of sale, the notaire is responsible for registering the property transfer with the local land registry, known as the "service de la publicité foncière." This registration process ensures that the buyer's ownership rights are officially recognized and protected, and that any potential legal issues or disputes related to the property are resolved before the transfer of ownership takes place.

The notaire will submit the necessary paperwork and pay any required registration fees on behalf of the buyer. Once the registration process is complete, the notaire will provide the buyer with a copy of the final deed of sale, as well as a certificate of property ownership, known as the "attestation de propriété."

Engaging the services of a notaire is a key step in the property buying process in France, and their expertise and guidance can help safeguard your interests and protect your investment. By understanding the role of the notaire and working closely with them throughout the transaction, you can ensure a successful property purchase and enjoy the benefits of property ownership in France.

□

LEGAL CHECKS AND DOCUMENTATION

When purchasing a property in France, there are several legal checks and documents that must be obtained, reviewed, and completed to ensure a smooth and legally compliant transaction. These checks and documents help to protect the buyer's interests, verify the property's legal status and ownership rights, and comply with French property law and regulations. In this section, we'll outline the key legal checks and documentation involved in the property buying process in France.

1. Land Registry Searches

One of the first legal checks to be performed when buying a property in France is a search of the local land registry, known as the "service de la publicité foncière." The land registry maintains records of all property transactions and ownership rights within a specific geographical area, and a search of these records can reveal crucial information about the property's history, boundaries, and any potential issues or disputes.

The notaire is responsible for conducting the land registry searches on behalf of the buyer, ensuring that the property's title is clear and free from any encumbrances or legal issues that could affect the transfer of ownership.

2. Property Diagnostic Reports

French property law requires sellers to provide a series of diagnostic reports on the property being sold, which cover various aspects such as the structural condition, energy efficiency, and potential hazards. These reports, collectively referred to as the "dossier de diagnostic technique" (DDT), must be provided to the buyer before the signing of the sale and purchase agreement.

Some of the key diagnostic reports included in the DDT are:

• Energy Performance Certificate (DPE): This report assesses the property's energy efficiency, providing a rating from A (most efficient) to G (least efficient).

• Lead Report (CREP): This report identifies any lead-based paint or materials within the property, which can be a health hazard, particularly for young children.

• Asbestos Report (DAPP): This report checks for the presence of asbestos in the property, which can pose a risk to health if disturbed or damaged.

• Termites Report (DT): This report looks for any signs of wood-destroying insects, such as termites, which can cause significant structural damage to a property.

• Natural and Technological Risks Report (ERNMT): This report outlines any potential risks related to natural or technological hazards, such as flooding, landslides, or industrial accidents, which could affect the property.

The buyer should carefully review these diagnostic reports and consider any potential issues or risks they may reveal before proceeding with the property purchase.

3. Sale and Purchase Agreement

The sale and purchase agreement, known as the "compromis de vente" or "promesse de vente," is a legally binding document that outlines the terms and conditions of the property sale. The notaire is responsible for preparing this document, ensuring that it accurately reflects the intentions of both the buyer and the seller and complies with French property law and regulations.

The sale and purchase agreement should include key information such as the agreed-upon purchase price, the completion date, and any special conditions or contingencies that must be met before the transaction can proceed. The buyer and seller must both sign the agreement, and a deposit, typically 10% of the purchase price, is paid by the buyer to secure the property.

4. Final Deed of Sale

Once the due diligence process is complete and all special conditions or contingencies have been met, the notaire will prepare the final deed of sale, known as the "acte de vente" or "acte authentique." This document formalizes the transfer of property ownership from the seller to the buyer and is legally binding upon both parties.

The final deed of sale should be reviewed carefully by the buyer and their legal representative to ensure that it accurately reflects the terms of the sale and purchase agreement and complies with all relevant French property laws and regulations. Once the final deed of sale is signed by both parties, the notaire will register the property transfer with the local land registry, and the buyer will become the official owner of the property.

5. Certificate of Property Ownership

Following the registration of the property transfer, the notaire will provide the buyer with a certificate of property ownership, known as the "attestation de propriété." This document serves as proof of the buyer's ownership rights and can be used for various purposes, such as registering with local authorities, obtaining utility services, or securing a mortgage.

By working closely with a notaire and ensuring that all required checks and documents are completed accurately and on time, you can safeguard your interests and enjoy a smooth property purchase experience.

□

IV: THE PROPERTY SEARCH

Embarking on the property search in France can be both exciting and challenging, as you navigate through various regions, property types, and budgets to find your dream home. To make the process easier, it's essential to define your priorities, such as location, size, and desired amenities. Online property portals, local real estate agents, and property exhibitions can be valuable resources in your search. Engaging a real estate agent with expertise in the French market can provide invaluable assistance, offering insights into local property trends, and helping to identify potential properties that meet your criteria. Remember to take your time and enjoy the journey to find your perfect French home.

□

STRATEGIES FOR FINDING YOUR DREAM PROPERTY

Searching for your dream property in France can be a thrilling yet overwhelming experience. With so many beautiful regions, property types, and styles to choose from, it's crucial to have a solid plan and implement effective strategies to find the perfect home. In this section, we will explore some proven strategies to help you navigate the French property market and find your dream property.

1. Define Your Priorities

Before starting your property search, take some time to define your priorities and establish your criteria for your dream home. Consider factors such as:

• Location: Which region, city, or town in France do you want to live in? Are you drawn to a particular climate, lifestyle, or cultural experience?

• Property type: Do you prefer a historic château, a chic city apartment, a rural farmhouse, or a modern villa?

• Size and layout: How many bedrooms and living spaces do you need? What kind of layout suits your lifestyle and preferences?

• Budget: Determine a realistic budget based on your financial situation and the property market trends in your desired area.

• Amenities and facilities: What amenities and facilities are essential to you? Proximity to shops, schools, healthcare, public transport, or recreational activities may be important factors.

• Renovation potential: Are you willing to undertake a renovation project, or do you prefer a move-in ready property?

By clearly defining your priorities, you'll be better equipped to focus your search and identify properties that truly align with your needs and desires.

2. Research the Market

Gain a solid understanding of the French property market by conducting thorough research. Investigate property trends, pricing, and market conditions in your desired area. Familiarize yourself with the various regions, their unique characteristics, and the types of properties available.

Consider attending French property exhibitions, subscribing to property magazines or newsletters, and joining online forums or social media groups where you can interact with other buyers and experts in the French property market. The more you know about the market, the better equipped you'll be to make informed decisions and find your dream property.

3. Utilize Online Property Portals

Online property portals have become an indispensable tool for property buyers, offering a wealth of information and listings to explore. French property portals such as Seloger, Green-Acres, and Rightmove provide a vast selection of property listings, often with detailed descriptions, photographs, and even virtual tours.

Take advantage of these portals to get a sense of the properties available in your desired area, and create a shortlist of potential properties that meet your criteria. Set up email alerts to receive updates on new listings and price reductions, ensuring you don't miss out on any opportunities.

4. Engage a Local Real Estate Agent

Working with a reputable local real estate agent can be invaluable in your property search. A good agent will have in-depth knowledge of the local property market, as well as access to exclusive listings not advertised on public portals.

Choose an agent with expertise in the French property market, and who understands your priorities and preferences. They can help to identify potential properties that meet your criteria, arrange viewings, and provide guidance on pricing and negotiation strategies.

5. Network with Locals and Expats

Establishing connections with locals and expats living in your desired area can be an excellent way to uncover off-market properties and gain insights into the local property market. Join local clubs, attend community events, or participate in online forums and social media groups to build your network.

Locals and expats may be aware of properties for sale that haven't been officially listed or may have inside knowledge of upcoming listings. Additionally, they can offer invaluable advice on the nuances of living in a particular area, helping you make a more informed decision about your property purchase.

6. Schedule Property Viewings

Once you've identified potential properties that meet your criteria, arrange property viewings to inspect them in person. While photographs and virtual tours can provide a good impression of a property, nothing can replace the experience of seeing it firsthand.

When viewing properties, take your time to assess each one carefully, considering factors such as its condition, layout, location, and potential for renovation or improvement. Make a list of questions to ask the seller or real estate agent, and take notes and photographs during the viewings to help you remember the details of each property.

7. Be Prepared to Act Quickly

The French property market can be competitive, particularly in popular areas, so it's essential to be prepared to act quickly when you find your dream property. Make sure you have your finances in order, with a clear understanding of your budget and the costs associated with purchasing a property in France.

If you're considering a mortgage, it's a good idea to obtain a mortgage pre-approval from a reputable lender, which will give you a clear indication of your borrowing capacity and make your offer more attractive to sellers.

8. Be Open to Compromise

While it's essential to have a clear vision of your dream property, it's also important to be open to compromise. You may not find a property that meets every single one of your criteria, but by being flexible and willing to make some concessions, you can still find a wonderful home that suits your needs and preferences.

Consider whether certain elements of your criteria are negotiable, such as the property's size, location, or condition. By being open to compromise, you'll have a greater range of properties to choose from and increase your chances of finding your dream home.

9. Stay Organized

With so many properties to consider and a wealth of information to process, it's crucial to stay organized during your property search. Develop a system for tracking the properties you've viewed, including notes, photographs, and any relevant documents or correspondence.

Create a checklist of your priorities and use it to evaluate each property you view, ensuring that you remain focused on your goals and make informed decisions.

10. Be Patient and Persistent

Finally, remember that finding your dream property in France may take time and persistence. The property market can be unpredictable, and you may need to view numerous properties before finding the perfect one.

Stay patient and focused on your goals, and don't be disheartened if your search takes longer than expected. By implementing these strategies and remaining persistent, you'll be well on your way to finding your dream property in France.

Finding your dream property in France involves a combination of thorough research, effective networking, and a clear understanding of your priorities. By implementing these strategies and working closely with a reputable real estate agent, you can navigate the French property market with confidence and ultimately find the perfect home to suit your needs and desires.

WORKING WITH ESTATE AGENTS AND PROPERTY FINDERS

Navigating the French property market can be a complex and time-consuming process, particularly for those unfamiliar with the local market or the French language. Engaging the services of estate agents and property finders can significantly streamline your property search, providing valuable expertise, guidance, and access to a wide range of properties that meet your criteria. In this section, we will explore the benefits of working with estate agents and property finders, and offer tips on how to choose the right professionals to help you find your dream property in France.

1. The Benefits of Working with Estate Agents

Estate agents play a vital role in the French property market, acting as intermediaries between buyers and sellers. They offer several key benefits for property buyers:

• **Local expertise:** Estate agents possess in-depth knowledge of the local property market, including property trends, pricing, and available inventory. They can provide valuable insights and advice on the best areas to search for properties based on your priorities and budget.

• **Access to properties:** Estate agents have access to a wide range of property listings, including exclusive properties not advertised on public portals. They can help you identify suitable properties that meet your criteria and arrange viewings on your behalf.

• **Negotiation and transaction support:** Estate agents are skilled negotiators who can assist you in making an offer, negotiating the purchase price, and handling the administrative aspects of the property transaction. They can also recommend other professionals, such as notaires, mortgage brokers, or surveyors, to support you throughout the buying process.

2. The Benefits of Working with Property Finders

Property finders, also known as buyer's agents or property search agents, offer a more specialized service tailored specifically to the needs of property buyers. They differ from estate agents in that they work exclusively on behalf of the buyer, rather than representing both buyers and sellers. Property finders offer several advantages:

- **Personalized service**: Property finders work closely with you to understand your specific needs, preferences, and budget. They then conduct a targeted property search on your behalf, saving you time and effort in the process.

- **Access to off-market properties:** Property finders often have connections with local estate agents, developers, and private sellers, allowing them to uncover off-market properties that may not be publicly advertised.

- **Independent advice:** As property finders represent only the buyer's interests, they can provide unbiased advice on the pros and cons of each property and help you make informed decisions throughout the purchasing process.

3. Choosing the Right Professional

To ensure a successful property search, it's essential to work with estate agents and property finders who possess the necessary expertise, local knowledge, and commitment to your best interests. Consider the following factors when selecting a professional to assist with your property search:

• **Reputation**: Seek recommendations from friends, family, or online forums, and research potential professionals' online presence and reviews.

• **Experience**: Choose professionals with a proven track record of success in the French property market, and who have experience working with foreign buyers.

• **Language skills**: If you're not fluent in French, it's important to work with professionals who can communicate effectively in your native language.

• **Specialization**: Select professionals who specialize in your desired property type or region, ensuring they have the necessary expertise to find the best properties for you.

• **Rapport**: Establish a good rapport with your chosen professionals, as you'll be working closely together throughout the property search process.

Working with estate agents and property finders can significantly enhance your property search experience, providing valuable expertise, guidance, and access to a wider range of properties. By carefully selecting professionals who possess the necessary skills, knowledge, and commitment to your best interests, you can navigate the French property market with confidence and ultimately find your dream property in France. Remember that building a strong relationship with your chosen professionals will ensure a smoother and more enjoyable property search experience, and ultimately help you find the perfect home to suit your needs and desires.

□

ONLINE RESOURCES FOR PROPERTY SEARCH

In today's digital age, the internet has become an essential tool for property buyers searching for their dream home in France. Online resources provide a wealth of information and property listings, making it easier than ever to research the market, compare properties, and narrow down your search. In this section, we'll explore some of the most useful online resources for your property search in France and offer tips on how to make the most of these platforms.

1. Property Portals

Property portals are an invaluable resource for property buyers, offering a vast selection of property listings across France. These platforms allow you to search for properties based on your desired location, property type, budget, and other criteria. Some popular French property portals include:

• **Seloger**: One of the largest property portals in France, Seloger offers a wide range of properties for sale, including apartments, houses, and luxury properties.

• **Green-Acres**: Specializing in rural properties, Green-Acres features a selection of homes in the French countryside, from charming farmhouses to historic châteaux.

• **Rightmove**: A popular UK-based property portal, Rightmove has an extensive range of French properties listed by both local and international estate agents.

Make use of these portals to browse available properties, create a shortlist of potential homes, and set up email alerts to receive updates on new listings and price reductions.

2. Estate Agent Websites

While property portals offer a comprehensive selection of properties, it's also worth visiting the websites of individual estate agents. Many agents list their properties on their own websites, sometimes before they appear on property portals. By regularly checking estate agent websites, you may be able to discover new properties before other buyers.

If you have a specific region or town in mind, search for local estate agents specializing in that area. Many agents offer detailed property descriptions, photographs, and even virtual tours, allowing you to get a good impression of the properties on offer.

3. Property Forums and Social Media Groups

Online forums and social media groups dedicated to the French property market can provide valuable insights, advice, and even property recommendations from fellow property buyers and industry experts. Join forums and groups related to your desired region or property type, and engage with the community to gather useful information and tips.

Examples of such forums and groups include:

• French Property Forum: A popular online forum covering various aspects of the French property market, including buying, selling, and renovation advice.

• Facebook groups: Search for Facebook groups focused on French property, such as "Living and Buying Property in France" or regional-specific groups like "Property in Provence."

4. Property Blogs and Newsletters

Following property blogs and subscribing to newsletters can help you stay up-to-date with the latest news, trends, and insights in the French property market. Many blogs and newsletters also feature property listings, renovation projects, and case studies that can inspire and inform your property search.

Examples of property blogs and newsletters include:

• French Property News: A leading property magazine and website, French Property News offers articles on buying, selling, and renovating properties in France, as well as a selection of property listings.

• The French Property Insider: A weekly newsletter published by Paris-based property expert Adrian Leeds, featuring property listings, market insights, and buying advice.

5. Property Videos and Virtual Tours

With the increasing use of technology in the property industry, many estate agents and property portals now offer video content and virtual tours of their listings. These resources can provide a more immersive and realistic experience of a property, allowing you to explore it in greater detail before arranging a viewing in person.

Making the most of the available online resources can significantly enhance your property search experience in France. By utilizing property portals, estate agent websites, forums, social media groups, blogs, newsletters, and property videos, you can access a wealth of information and property listings to help you find your dream home. Stay proactive and organized in your search, and be prepared to act quickly when you find the perfect property that meets your needs and desires. By leveraging these online resources, you'll be well on your way to successfully navigating the French property market and securing your dream home in France.

CONDUCTING PROPERTY VIEWINGS AND EVALUATIONS

Once you've identified potential properties through your online search, estate agent recommendations, or property finders, the next crucial step is to conduct property viewings and evaluations. Visiting properties in person allows you to gain a deeper understanding of their condition, location, and potential, helping you make an informed decision on whether to proceed with an offer. In this section, we'll explore how to effectively conduct property viewings and evaluations, including what to look for, what questions to ask, and how to compare properties.

1. Prepare for Property Viewings

Before attending property viewings, it's essential to be well-prepared to make the most of your time and ensure a thorough evaluation. Consider the following tips:

• **Create a viewing schedule:** If you're planning to view multiple properties in one trip, create a schedule that includes the property address, appointment time, and contact details for the estate agent or seller. This will help you stay organized and ensure you don't miss any viewings.

• **Bring a notebook or digital device**: Take notes during your property viewings, as this will help you remember key details and make comparisons between properties easier.

• **Bring a camera or smartphone**: Take photographs of each property to help you recall specific features and visualize the space after the viewing.

2. Conducting the Viewing

During the property viewing, keep the following considerations in mind:

• **First impressions:** Pay attention to your initial reaction to the property, as this can provide valuable insight into whether it's the right fit for you. Consider the property's curb appeal, the surrounding neighborhood, and the atmosphere of the home.

• **Property layout and flow**: Assess the property's layout, room sizes, and flow. Determine whether the space is functional and suits your lifestyle, or if any renovations or alterations would be necessary to make it work for you.

• **Natural light and ventilation**: Check the amount of natural light and ventilation in each room. Properties with good natural light and airflow are not only more comfortable to live in but can also help reduce energy costs.

• **Condition and maintenance**: Examine the property's general condition, including signs of dampness, cracks, or structural issues. Assess the state of the roof, plumbing, and electrical systems, and consider whether any repairs or upgrades would be required.

• **Outdoor space**: If the property has a garden or outdoor area, consider how it meets your needs in terms of size, privacy, and maintenance.

3. Ask the Right Questions

When viewing a property, it's important to ask the estate agent or seller relevant questions to gather valuable information about the property. Some essential questions to ask include:

• How long has the property been on the market?

• Have there been any offers on the property?

• Why is the owner selling the property?

• Are there any known issues with the property, such as structural problems, disputes with neighbors, or legal issues?

• What is the property's energy performance rating?

• What are the annual property taxes and utility costs?

4. Evaluating the Location

The location of your property is a crucial factor to consider when making a purchase. Assess the property's location in terms of:

• **Proximity to amenities**: Consider the property's proximity to essential amenities, such as shops, schools, healthcare facilities, and public transportation. This can impact your daily life and the property's resale value.

• **Safety and security**: Evaluate the safety and security of the neighborhood, including crime rates and the presence of security measures, such as surveillance cameras or gated communities.

• **Noise and pollution:** Assess the level of noise and pollution in the area, particularly if the property is near busy roads or industrial sites.

5. Comparing Properties

After conducting several property viewings, compare the properties based on your notes, photographs, and impressions. Create a list of pros and cons for each property to help you evaluate them objectively. Consider factors such as:

• **Price**: Compare the properties based on their asking price and your budget. Consider the cost of any necessary repairs or renovations and whether the property represents good value for money.

• **Condition**: Assess the overall condition of each property, including the structure, interior, and exterior. Determine the level of work required and whether you're willing and able to undertake it.

• **Location**: Compare the properties' locations in terms of access to amenities, safety, and future growth potential. Keep in mind that a property in a desirable location may hold its value better and be easier to sell in the future.

• **Size and layout**: Compare the size and layout of the properties, considering how well they accommodate your needs and preferences. This may include the number of bedrooms and bathrooms, storage space, and outdoor areas.

• **Potential for improvements**: Consider the potential for improvements or extensions that could add value to the property or enhance your lifestyle. This may include adding a swimming pool, converting a loft, or extending the living area.

6. Second Viewings and Professional Assessments

Once you've narrowed down your selection, it's a good idea to arrange for second viewings of your top choices. This allows you to revisit the properties with a fresh perspective and ensure that your initial impressions were accurate. It's also an opportunity to ask any additional questions or clarify any concerns.

In addition to conducting your evaluations, it's advisable to enlist the help of professionals to assess the property before making an offer. This may include:

• **A structural survey**: A professional surveyor can conduct a thorough assessment of the property's structure and identify any potential issues, such as subsidence, dampness, or roof problems.

• **A property valuation:** A professional valuation can help you determine the property's market value, ensuring that you're paying a fair price and making a wise investment.

• **Legal checks**: Consult a lawyer or notaire to verify the property's legal status, including ownership, planning permissions, and any potential disputes or restrictions.

By conducting thorough property viewings and evaluations, asking the right questions, and comparing your options, you'll be well-equipped to make an informed decision on your French property purchase. Don't be afraid to take your time and seek professional advice, as this will help you find the perfect property that meets your needs, preferences, and budget.

□

V: MAKING AN OFFER AND NEGOTIATING

After conducting thorough property viewings and evaluations, the next step is to make an offer and negotiate with the seller. Begin by determining a fair offer price based on the property's condition, location, and market value. Consult your estate agent or a professional valuer for guidance. When presenting your offer, be prepared to explain your reasoning and provide evidence to support your price. Be open to negotiations and remain flexible, but also set a maximum budget to avoid overstretching your finances. Maintain clear communication with the seller or their agent throughout the process to ensure a smooth and successful negotiation.

PREPARING AND SUBMITTING AN OFFER

Once you've found the perfect property and decided to make an offer, it's essential to prepare and submit a well-considered proposal to the seller. A well-prepared offer can not only increase your chances of acceptance but also set the stage for a smooth negotiation and transaction process. Follow these steps to effectively prepare and submit an offer on a French property:

1. Determine Your Offer Price

The first step in preparing an offer is to determine a fair price based on your research and evaluation of the property. Consider factors such as:

• The property's condition, including the cost of any necessary repairs or renovations

• The location and its impact on the property's value

• Comparable property sales in the area

• The current state of the French property market

• Your personal budget and financial circumstances

It's a good idea to consult with your estate agent or a professional valuer for guidance on determining an appropriate offer price.

2. Prepare Your Offer Letter

Once you've decided on an offer price, prepare a formal offer letter to submit to the seller or their agent. Your offer letter should include:

• A clear statement of your offer price, in both words and figures

• The property's address and a brief description

• Any conditions or contingencies attached to your offer, such as obtaining financing or selling your current property

• Your desired completion date and timeframe for the transaction

• A request for a response by a specific date, to encourage timely communication

Be sure to sign and date your offer letter and make a copy for your records.

3. Gather Supporting Documentation

To demonstrate your seriousness and financial capability, gather supporting documentation to submit with your offer. This may include:

• Proof of funds: A bank statement or letter from your financial institution confirming your ability to cover the purchase price and associated costs

• Mortgage pre-approval: A letter from your mortgage lender confirming that you've been pre-approved for a loan, if applicable

• Personal identification: A copy of your passport or other valid ID to verify your identity

4. Submit Your Offer

Submit your offer letter and supporting documentation to the seller or their agent, either in person, by mail, or via email. It's a good idea to follow up with a phone call to confirm receipt and discuss any questions or concerns.

5. Be Prepared for Negotiation

Once you've submitted your offer, be prepared for the possibility of negotiation. The seller may counter your offer with a higher price or different terms, and it's essential to remain flexible and open to compromise. Keep in mind your maximum budget and be prepared to walk away if the negotiation doesn't align with your financial limitations or goals.

6. Confirm Acceptance in Writing

If the seller accepts your offer, obtain written confirmation to avoid any misunderstandings or disputes later in the transaction process. This can be in the form of a signed and dated acceptance letter or a formal sales agreement (compromis de vente) prepared by a notaire.

By following these steps to prepare and submit a well-considered offer, you'll increase your chances of a successful negotiation and purchase of your dream French property. Remember to consult with professionals, such as estate agents, valuers, and legal advisors, throughout the process to ensure you're making informed decisions and navigating the French property market with confidence.

□

UNDERSTANDING AND NEGOTIATING THE COMPROMIS DE VENTE

The compromis de vente, also known as the preliminary sales agreement, is a legally binding document that outlines the terms and conditions of the property sale between the buyer and the seller in France. This critical document serves as the foundation for the entire property transaction process, and it's essential to understand and negotiate its contents to ensure a successful purchase. In this section, we'll explore the key elements of the compromis de vente and provide guidance on how to negotiate its terms effectively.

1. Key Elements of the Compromis de Vente

The compromis de vente typically includes the following information:

• The property's description, including its address, size, and any attached land or outbuildings

• The agreed-upon purchase price and any related fees, such as notary fees and taxes

• The buyer's and seller's personal details, including names, addresses, and identification numbers

• The deposit amount, usually 5-10% of the purchase price, to be paid by the buyer upon signing the agreement

• Any conditions or contingencies attached to the sale, such as obtaining financing, completing inspections, or obtaining planning permissions

• The anticipated completion date, usually 2-3 months after signing the compromis de vente

• The notaire's details, who will prepare and oversee the final sales contract (acte de vente)

2. Reviewing and Understanding the Agreement

Before signing the compromis de vente, it's essential to thoroughly review and understand its contents. Ensure that all the information is accurate and complete, and consult with a notaire, lawyer, or estate agent for guidance if needed. Remember that the compromis de vente is a legally binding document, and signing it commits you to purchasing the property under the agreed-upon terms.

3. Negotiating the Terms

While many aspects of the compromis de vente may be standard, certain elements can be negotiated to better align with your preferences and requirements. Some negotiable items may include:

• The purchase price: If you haven't already agreed upon a price during the initial offer stage, this is your opportunity to negotiate with the seller.

• The deposit amount: While the standard deposit is typically 5-10% of the purchase price, you may be able to negotiate a higher or lower amount depending on your financial situation and the seller's preferences.

• Contingencies and conditions: You may wish to include specific conditions or contingencies in the compromis de vente, such as obtaining a mortgage, completing a satisfactory structural survey, or obtaining planning permission for renovations.

• Completion date: Although the completion date is generally set for 2-3 months after signing the compromis de vente, you may be able to negotiate a different timeline if it better suits your needs.

4. Seeking Professional Advice

Given the legal and financial implications of the compromis de vente, it's advisable to seek professional advice throughout the negotiation process. Consult with a notaire, lawyer, or estate agent who is experienced in French property transactions to ensure that your interests are protected and that the agreement aligns with your needs and goals.

5. Signing the Agreement

Once you and the seller have agreed upon the terms of the compromis de vente and any necessary revisions have been made, both parties will sign the document in the presence of a notaire. The buyer will typically pay the agreed-upon deposit at this stage, and the agreement becomes legally binding.

Understanding and negotiating the compromis de vente is a critical step in the French property buying process. By reviewing the agreement carefully, negotiating key terms, and seeking professional advice, you can protect your interests and ensure a successful property transaction that meets your needs and goals.

□

CONTINGENCIES AND CONDITIONS TO PROTECT YOUR INTERESTS

When purchasing a property in France, it's crucial to include contingencies and conditions in the compromis de vente (preliminary sales agreement) to protect your interests and minimize risks. These provisions allow you to withdraw from the agreement without penalties if certain requirements are not met, ensuring a more secure and satisfactory property transaction. In this section, we'll discuss key contingencies and conditions you may consider including in the compromis de vente to safeguard your interests.

1. Mortgage Contingency

One of the most common contingencies in a property purchase is a mortgage contingency, which states that the sale is dependent on your ability to secure financing. If you're unable to obtain a mortgage within a specified timeframe, this contingency allows you to back out of the agreement without forfeiting your deposit. Ensure that the compromis de vente clearly states the mortgage amount, interest rate, and deadline for securing financing to provide you with adequate protection.

2. Property Inspection and Survey Contingency

Including a property inspection and survey contingency in the compromis de vente is essential for identifying any potential structural or maintenance issues that could affect the property's value or require costly repairs. This contingency allows you to withdraw from the agreement or renegotiate the purchase price if the inspection or survey uncovers significant problems. Specify a deadline for completing the inspections and surveys, as well as the type of inspections required (e.g., structural survey, pest inspection, or electrical and plumbing inspections).

3. Planning Permission Contingency

If you plan to undertake significant renovations, extensions, or other modifications to the property, a planning permission contingency can protect you from potential legal issues and financial losses. This provision makes the sale dependent on obtaining the necessary planning permissions from the local authorities. Ensure that the compromis de vente outlines the specific permissions required, the deadline for obtaining them, and the consequences if the permissions are not granted (e.g., withdrawal from the agreement or renegotiation of the purchase price).

4. Sale of Existing Property Contingency

If your ability to purchase the French property depends on selling your current home, consider including a sale of existing property contingency. This provision allows you to withdraw from the agreement without penalties if you're unable to sell your existing property within a specified timeframe. Be sure to clearly state the deadline for selling your property and any related conditions, such as a minimum acceptable sale price.

5. Clear Title Contingency

A clear title contingency ensures that the seller has the legal right to sell the property and that there are no outstanding claims or encumbrances on the title, such as liens, easements, or boundary disputes. This provision protects you from potential legal issues and financial losses related to title disputes. The compromis de vente should outline the responsibility of the seller to provide a clear title and the process for resolving any title issues that may arise.

Consult with a notaire, lawyer, or estate agent experienced in French property transactions to ensure that your compromis de vente adequately safeguards your interests and provides you with the necessary protection throughout the home buying process.

COOLING-OFF PERIOD AND WITHDRAWAL RIGHTS

In France, the property buying process includes a cooling-off period and withdrawal rights to protect the buyer and provide an opportunity to reconsider their decision without significant financial penalties. Understanding these rights and how they apply to your property purchase is essential for a successful and stress-free transaction. In this section, we'll explore the cooling-off period and withdrawal rights in the French property buying process.

1. The Cooling-Off Period

The cooling-off period, known as the "délai de rétractation," is a mandatory 10-day period during which the buyer can change their mind and withdraw from the property purchase without any penalties. This period begins the day after the buyer receives a copy of the signed compromis de vente (preliminary sales agreement) by registered mail, hand delivery, or electronic means with acknowledgment of receipt.

During the cooling-off period, the buyer can decide to cancel the purchase for any reason or even no reason at all. The buyer is not required to provide justification for their decision or pay any penalties for withdrawing from the sale.

2. Exercising Your Withdrawal Rights

To exercise your withdrawal rights during the cooling-off period, you must notify the seller and the notaire in writing, either by registered mail with acknowledgment of receipt or hand delivery against receipt. The notification must be sent before the end of the 10-day period to be valid. It's essential to keep proof of the date of dispatch or delivery to avoid any disputes regarding the timeliness of your withdrawal.

Once you've notified the seller and notaire of your decision to withdraw, the sale is considered null and void. If you've already paid a deposit, it must be refunded to you in full within 21 days from the receipt of your withdrawal notification.

3. Exceptions to the Cooling-Off Period

It's important to note that the cooling-off period does not apply to all property transactions in France. Some exceptions include:

• The purchase of a commercial property, a plot of land without a construction permit, or a new property directly from a developer or builder

• The purchase of a property at a public auction

• The purchase of a property by a professional real estate investor or a company

In these cases, the buyer may not benefit from a cooling-off period or withdrawal rights, and the terms of the compromis de vente will dictate the conditions and penalties for withdrawing from the sale.

4. Withdrawal Rights Beyond the Cooling-Off Period

If you wish to withdraw from the property purchase after the cooling-off period has passed, you may still do so if certain conditions or contingencies specified in the compromis de vente have not been met. For instance, if you're unable to secure a mortgage, obtain necessary planning permissions, or if the property inspection reveals significant issues, you can withdraw from the sale without penalties, provided that these contingencies were included in the agreement.

By understanding the cooling-off period and withdrawal rights in the French property buying process, you can make more informed decisions and feel confident knowing that you have the opportunity to reconsider your purchase without facing significant financial penalties. Always consult with a notaire, lawyer, or estate agent experienced in French property transactions to ensure that your interests are protected throughout the process.

□

VI: THE PROPERTY PURCHASE PROCESS

The property purchase process in France involves several key steps that ensure a smooth and legally sound transaction. Beginning with a thorough property search and working with estate agents or property finders, you'll identify your dream property and make an offer. Upon agreement, you'll sign the compromis de vente, which outlines the terms and conditions of the sale. The cooling-off period and contingencies offer protection and withdrawal rights for the buyer. Next, the notaire conducts legal checks, and you secure financing through a mortgage or other means. Finally, the acte de vente is signed, transferring ownership and concluding the purchase.

THE ROLE OF THE NOTAIRE IN THE PURCHASE PROCESS

In France, the notaire plays a crucial role in the property purchase process, ensuring the transaction is legally sound and properly registered. As an impartial public official, the notaire represents both the buyer and the seller, acting as a mediator and advisor throughout the process. In this section, we'll discuss the key responsibilities and duties of the notaire in the French property purchase process.

1. Drafting the Compromis de Vente

The notaire is responsible for drafting the compromis de vente (preliminary sales agreement), which outlines the terms and conditions of the property sale. This document includes information such as the agreed-upon price, the completion date, and any contingencies or conditions that must be met before the sale can proceed. The notaire ensures that the compromis de vente is legally binding and adheres to French property laws.

2. Conducting Legal Checks

Once the compromis de vente is signed, the notaire conducts various legal checks to ensure a smooth and legally sound transaction. This includes verifying the seller's ownership and ensuring there are no outstanding debts or claims on the property, as well as conducting land registry searches and checking for any easements or restrictions that could affect the property's use or value. These checks help protect the buyer from potential legal issues and financial losses.

3. Managing Financial Transactions

The notaire is responsible for managing the financial aspects of the property purchase, including the payment of the deposit, the balance of the purchase price, and any taxes or fees associated with the transaction. They ensure that all funds are transferred securely and in accordance with French property law.

4. Preparing and Registering the Acte de Vente

After all legal checks are completed and financing is secured, the notaire prepares the acte de vente (final sales contract), which transfers ownership of the property from the seller to the buyer. Both parties sign the acte de vente in the presence of the notaire, who then registers the transaction with the French land registry, ensuring that the property's ownership is properly recorded and legally binding.

5. Advising on Tax and Inheritance Issues

Finally, the notaire advises both the buyer and the seller on tax and inheritance issues related to the property transaction. They can help the buyer understand the tax implications of owning a property in France and provide guidance on estate planning and inheritance laws.

The notaire plays a pivotal role in the French property purchase process, ensuring that the transaction is legally sound and properly registered. By working closely with the notaire, buyers can have peace of mind knowing that their property purchase is in good hands and that their interests are protected throughout the process.

PREPARING FOR THE ACTE DE VENTE

The acte de vente, or final sales contract, is a crucial document that legally transfers the ownership of a property from the seller to the buyer in France. Preparing for the acte de vente involves several important steps that ensure the transaction proceeds smoothly and according to French property law. In this section, we'll outline the steps to prepare for the acte de vente.

1. Satisfying Contingencies and Conditions

Before the acte de vente can be signed, all contingencies and conditions outlined in the compromis de vente must be satisfied. This may include obtaining a mortgage, securing necessary planning permissions, or addressing any issues identified during property inspections. Both the buyer and the seller are responsible for fulfilling their respective obligations before moving forward with the acte de vente.

2. Obtaining a Mortgage

If you're financing the property purchase with a mortgage, it's essential to finalize your mortgage application and obtain a mortgage approval before the acte de vente can be signed. This process typically involves providing your lender with the necessary documentation, such as proof of income, bank statements, and credit reports. Once your mortgage is approved, the lender will issue a mortgage offer, which outlines the terms and conditions of the loan.

3. Preparing the Final Sales Contract

The notaire is responsible for drafting the acte de vente, which includes all the necessary information regarding the property, the buyer, the seller, and the agreed-upon terms of the transaction. The notaire will ensure that the acte de vente is legally sound and adheres to French property laws. Before signing the acte de vente, it's essential to review the document thoroughly, ensuring that all the details are accurate and consistent with the compromis de vente.

4. Arranging for Payment

Before the signing of the acte de vente, the buyer must arrange for the payment of the remaining balance of the purchase price, along with any additional fees and taxes associated with the transaction. The notaire typically manages the financial transactions, ensuring that funds are transferred securely and in accordance with French property law.

5. Signing the Acte de Vente

With all contingencies satisfied, the mortgage approved, and the acte de vente prepared, both the buyer and the seller will meet with the notaire to sign the final sales contract. This is a critical moment in the property purchase process, as the acte de vente legally transfers ownership of the property from the seller to the buyer. Once signed, the notaire will register the transaction with the French land registry, ensuring that the property's ownership is properly recorded and legally binding.

Preparing for the acte de vente is a crucial part of the French property purchase process. By satisfying contingencies, finalizing your mortgage, reviewing the final sales contract, and arranging for payment, you'll be well-prepared to complete the transaction and take ownership of your new property in France.

UNDERSTANDING PROPERTY SURVEYS AND INSPECTIONS

In France, property surveys and inspections are essential steps in the home-buying process to ensure that you are making an informed decision and protecting your investment. These assessments help identify potential issues or concerns with the property, providing buyers with valuable information before finalizing the purchase. Here, we'll discuss the importance of property surveys and inspections, and what to expect during the process.

1. Types of Surveys and Inspections

There are various types of surveys and inspections that can be conducted on a property in France, depending on the age and condition of the property, as well as the buyer's specific concerns. Some common surveys and inspections include:

• Structural surveys: Assess the overall condition of the building, checking for structural defects, dampness, and other potential problems.

• Pest inspections: Identify any signs of pest infestations, such as termites or wood-boring insects, which could cause significant damage to the property.

• Energy performance assessments: Evaluate the property's energy efficiency and provide recommendations for improvements.

2. Diagnostics Techniques Immobiliers (DTI)

French law requires sellers to provide a series of mandatory property inspections, known as Diagnostics Techniques Immobiliers (DTI), which cover various aspects, such as lead, asbestos, gas, electricity, and energy performance. These reports provide crucial information on the property's condition and help buyers make an informed decision.

3. The Importance of Surveys and Inspections

Property surveys and inspections provide valuable information on the property's condition, helping buyers identify potential issues and negotiate a fair price. They also allow buyers to plan for any necessary repairs or renovations, ensuring that their new home is safe and comfortable. In addition, some mortgage lenders may require specific surveys or inspections before approving a loan, making these assessments a critical part of the property purchase process.

Property surveys and inspections are essential steps in buying a house in France, offering valuable insight into the property's condition and ensuring a sound investment. By understanding the different types of assessments and their importance, you'll be well-prepared to make an informed decision when purchasing your dream property in France.

□

FINALIZING THE SALE AND TRANSFERRING OWNERSHIP

The final stage of the property purchase process in France involves finalizing the sale and transferring ownership from the seller to the buyer. This crucial step ensures a legally sound transaction and the successful completion of the purchase. In this section, we'll discuss the key aspects of finalizing the sale and transferring ownership of a property in France.

1. Signing the Acte de Vente

The acte de vente, or final sales contract, is the document that legally transfers ownership of the property from the seller to the buyer. Once all contingencies and conditions have been met, the mortgage has been approved, and the notaire has completed the necessary legal checks, both parties will meet with the notaire to sign the acte de vente. It's essential to review the document thoroughly before signing, ensuring that all the details are accurate and consistent with the compromis de vente.

2. Payment of the Purchase Price

Prior to the signing of the acte de vente, the buyer must arrange for the payment of the remaining balance of the purchase price, along with any additional fees and taxes associated with the transaction. The notaire typically manages the financial transactions, ensuring that funds are transferred securely and in accordance with French property law.

3. Registration of the Property Transfer

After the acte de vente has been signed, the notaire is responsible for registering the property transfer with the

French land registry. This registration process ensures that the property's ownership is properly recorded and legally binding. The notaire will also ensure that any outstanding taxes, fees, or other charges associated with the property are settled before the transfer is finalized.

4. Obtaining the Title Deed

Once the property transfer has been registered with the French land registry, the notaire will provide the buyer with a copy of the title deed, which serves as proof of ownership. This document includes important information about the property, such as its legal description, the names of the owners, and any easements or restrictions that may apply.

5. Handover of Keys and Possession

With the acte de vente signed and the property transfer registered, the seller will hand over the keys to the buyer, granting them possession of the property. At this point, the buyer can take occupancy of their new home and begin making any necessary repairs, renovations, or improvements.

6. Post-Sale Obligations

Even after the sale has been finalized and ownership transferred, both the buyer and the seller may have ongoing obligations related to the property. For example, the buyer may need to inform utility companies of the change in ownership and set up new accounts in their name. The seller, on the other hand, may need to provide the buyer with certain warranties or guarantees, such as those related to hidden defects or the proper functioning of appliances.

Finalizing the sale and transferring ownership of a property in France is a critical step in the home-buying process. By signing the acte de vente, arranging for payment, and registering the property transfer, buyers can ensure a smooth and legally sound transaction. With the keys in hand and the title deed as proof of ownership, they can then enjoy their new home and embrace the French lifestyle.

□

VII: MOVING TO FRANCE

Relocating to France is an exciting opportunity to immerse yourself in a new culture, language, and way of life. To make the most of this experience, it's essential to plan and prepare for your move. Begin by researching the region you'll be living in, understanding the local customs, and familiarizing yourself with the French language. Organize your finances, making sure you have access to necessary funds for your relocation and ongoing living expenses. Arrange for the transportation of your belongings and consider hiring a reputable moving company. Finally, ensure you have the appropriate visas, residency permits, or other necessary documentation to live and work in France legally. Embrace the adventure and enjoy your new life in your dream home.

NAVIGATING THE FRENCH RESIDENCY PROCESS

When moving to France, one of the most critical aspects to consider is obtaining the appropriate residency status. This process can be complex and time-consuming, but understanding the requirements and following the necessary steps will help ensure a smooth transition. In this section, we'll outline the key elements of navigating the French residency process.

1. Determine Your Residency Status

The first step in navigating the French residency process is to determine your residency status based on your nationality and the purpose of your stay.

• European Union (EU), European Economic Area (EEA), and Swiss citizens: If you are an EU, EEA, or Swiss citizen, you can live, work, and study in France without the need for a visa or residency permit. However, after three months of residence, you may need to register with your local town hall (mairie) or préfecture.

• Non-EU/EEA/Swiss citizens: If you are a citizen of a non-EU/EEA/Swiss country, you will generally need a visa and/or residency permit to live, work, or study in France.

2. Obtain the Appropriate Visa

For non-EU/EEA/Swiss citizens, the appropriate visa must be obtained before entering France. There are several types of visas, depending on the purpose and duration of your stay:

• Short-stay visas: For stays up to 90 days, such as tourism, business trips, or family visits.

• Long-stay visas: For stays longer than 90 days, which may include work, study, or family reunification purposes.

To apply for a French visa, you will typically need to submit an application to the French consulate or embassy in your home country, providing the necessary documentation and fees. The processing time for visas varies depending on the type and individual circumstances.

3. Apply for a Residency Permit (Carte de Séjour)

Once in France, non-EU/EEA/Swiss citizens with a long-stay visa will need to apply for a residency permit (carte de séjour) at the préfecture or sub-prefecture closest to their place of residence. This should be done within the first two months of arriving in France. Some long-stay visas may also serve as a residency permit (visa de long séjour valant titre de séjour, or VLS-TS), in which case, you will only need to validate your visa upon arrival.

When applying for a residency permit, you will need to provide documentation related to your identity, address, financial resources, health insurance, and the purpose of your stay (e.g., employment contract, enrollment in a study program, or proof of family ties). The specific requirements and fees may vary depending on the type of residency permit.

4. Renewing Your Residency Permit

Residency permits in France are typically issued for a duration of one to four years, depending on the type and individual circumstances. It's essential to renew your permit before it expires, and the renewal process should be initiated at least two months before the expiration date. You will need to provide updated documentation and pay the applicable fees.

5. Applying for Permanent Residency

After living in France for a certain period (usually five years), you may be eligible to apply for permanent residency, which grants you the right to live and work in France indefinitely. To qualify for permanent residency, you will need to demonstrate a stable income, adequate housing, and integration into French society (e.g., language skills, civic knowledge, and employment history). Permanent residency permits are typically valid for ten years and can be renewed indefinitely.

6. Acquiring French Citizenship

For those interested in becoming a French citizen, the naturalization process typically requires living in France for at least five years (this duration may be shorter in some cases, such as marriage to a French citizen or having French parents). In addition to the residency requirement, you will need to demonstrate fluency in the French language, knowledge of French history and culture, and good moral character.

Applying for French citizenship involves submitting a dossier to the préfecture, which includes documentation related to your identity, residence, employment, and integration into French society. If your application is approved, you will be invited to attend a naturalization ceremony, where you will take an oath of allegiance and receive your French nationality certificate.

7. Family Members and Dependents

If you have family members or dependents who will be joining you in France, you will need to ensure that they also have the appropriate visas and residency permits. This may involve applying for a family reunification visa, obtaining a separate residency permit for your spouse or children, or including them as dependents on your own residency application.

It's essential to research the specific requirements for family members and dependents, as they may vary depending on their nationality, age, and relationship to you.

8. Staying Informed and Seeking Professional Assistance

Navigating the French residency process can be challenging, particularly for those unfamiliar with the language and legal system. To ensure a smooth transition, it's essential to stay informed about the latest immigration rules, regulations, and procedures. This may involve consulting official government websites, attending information sessions, or joining expat communities for support and advice.

In some cases, you may wish to seek professional assistance from an immigration lawyer, relocation consultant, or other experts who can help guide you through the process and ensure that your application is complete and compliant.

Successfully navigating the French residency process requires careful planning, preparation, and attention to detail. By understanding the requirements for your specific situation, obtaining the necessary visas and permits, and following the appropriate procedures, you can embark on your new life in France with confidence and peace of mind.

□

LEARNING THE FRENCH LANGUAGE AND INTEGRATING INTO LOCAL CULTURE

Moving to France offers a unique opportunity to immerse yourself in a rich and diverse culture. Learning the French language and integrating into the local culture are essential aspects of making the most of your new life in France. In this section, we will explore strategies for learning the language and embracing the French way of life.

1. Language Learning Options

There are various methods to learn French, and you can choose the approach that best suits your needs, preferences, and learning style. Some popular options include:

• Language classes: Enroll in language courses at a local language school, university, or community center. Group classes provide a structured learning environment, opportunities for practice, and feedback from experienced teachers.

• Private tutoring: Hire a private tutor for personalized, one-on-one instruction tailored to your specific needs and goals. This option is typically more flexible and can help you progress more quickly.

• Language exchange: Partner with a native French speaker who is interested in learning your language, and practice together through conversation and language exchange activities.

• Online courses and apps: Utilize online language learning platforms and apps, such as Duolingo, Babbel, or Rosetta Stone, to learn at your own pace and convenience.

• Immersion: Immerse yourself in the French language by living with a French-speaking family, participating in cultural activities, or traveling to different regions of France.

2. Practice Makes Perfect

To become proficient in French, regular practice is essential. Incorporate the language into your daily life by:

• Engaging in conversations with native speakers, neighbors, and colleagues

• Watching French films, television shows, or YouTube videos

• Listening to French radio stations, podcasts, or audiobooks

• Reading French books, newspapers, or online articles

• Attending local language meetups, conversation groups, or cultural events

3. Embrace French Culture

Beyond language learning, integrating into French culture is vital for a fulfilling and successful life in France. Some ways to immerse yourself in the local culture include:

• Learn about French history and traditions: Develop an understanding of France's rich history, regional customs, and local traditions by visiting museums, historical sites, or attending cultural events and festivals.

• Enjoy French cuisine: Discover the diverse and delicious world of French cuisine by dining at local restaurants, visiting markets, or taking cooking classes to learn how to prepare traditional dishes.

• Appreciate French art, music, and literature: Explore France's cultural contributions by visiting art galleries, attending concerts, or reading classic French literature.

• Participate in local events and activities: Get involved in your community by attending local events, joining clubs or sports teams, or volunteering for local organizations.

4. Understand and Respect Social Etiquette

To fully integrate into French society, it's essential to understand and respect local social norms and etiquette. Some key points to keep in mind include:

• Greeting others with a polite "Bonjour" (hello) or "Bonsoir" (good evening) and always using "vous" (formal) until invited to use the informal "tu."

• Kissing on the cheek (la bise) is a common greeting among friends and acquaintances, but the number of kisses and the starting side can vary by region.

• Dining etiquette is essential in France, and it's crucial to respect table manners, such as using utensils correctly, keeping your hands visible, and waiting for the host to begin eating.

• Punctuality is valued in professional settings but may be more relaxed in social situations.

5. Be Patient and Persistent

Learning a new language and adapting to a different culture takes time and effort. It's important to be patient with yourself and persistent in your efforts to learn French and integrate into the local culture. Set realistic goals, celebrate your progress, and don't be afraid to make mistakes – they are a natural part of the learning process.

In conclusion, learning the French language and embracing the local culture are essential aspects of making the most of your new life in France. By exploring various language learning options, engaging in regular practice, immersing yourself in French culture, and understanding social etiquette, you will be well on your way to integrating into your new community and enjoying all that France has to offer. Remember to be patient and persistent in your efforts, and you'll find that the rewards of adapting to a new culture are well worth the challenges you may face along the way.

HEALTHCARE, EDUCATION, AND OTHER ESSENTIAL SERVICES IN FRANCE

Moving to France involves not only learning the language and integrating into the local culture but also navigating the country's healthcare, education, and other essential services. This section provides an overview of these services and offers guidance on how to access and make the most of them.

1. Healthcare System

France boasts an excellent healthcare system, ranked among the best in the world. The French healthcare system, known as L'Assurance Maladie, is a universal, public system funded through social security contributions and taxes. It provides comprehensive coverage for both residents and visitors, with most healthcare costs reimbursed at a high percentage.

a. Accessing Healthcare Services

To access healthcare services in France, you need to be registered with the French social security system. Once registered, you will receive a personal health insurance card called the Carte Vitale, which you must present at medical appointments, pharmacies, or hospitals.

For non-emergency medical care, you will generally need to make an appointment with a general practitioner (médecin généraliste) or a specialist (médecin spécialiste). In case of an emergency, you can go directly to the nearest hospital or call the emergency services at 15 (SAMU) or 112 (European emergency number).

b. Public vs. Private Healthcare

While the public healthcare system in France is of high quality, you may also choose to seek private healthcare services. Many expats opt for private health insurance (mutuelle) to cover any additional expenses not covered by the public system, such as dental and optical care or private hospital rooms.

c. Prescription Medications

Pharmacies in France are widespread and easily identifiable by the green cross sign. Prescription medications are usually subsidized, with the cost covered by your Carte Vitale and your mutuelle, if applicable. Over-the-counter medications are also available but may be more expensive than in other countries.

2. Education System

The French education system is well-regarded and offers a variety of options for both local and international students. Education in France is compulsory for children aged 6 to 16 and is divided into three main stages: primary (école), secondary (collège), and high school (lycée). Public schools are free of charge, and the academic year typically runs from September to July.

a. Public Schools

French public schools follow a national curriculum, and the language of instruction is predominantly French. To enroll your child in a public school, you will need to contact the local town hall (mairie) or the school directly. While public schools offer a high standard of education, the language barrier may be a challenge for non-French-speaking children.

b. International Schools

International schools are an excellent option for expat families, as they offer a more familiar curriculum and often teach in English or other languages. These schools typically follow the British, American, or International Baccalaureate curriculum and cater to a diverse student population. However, international schools are privately funded and can be expensive.

c. Bilingual Schools

Bilingual schools offer a middle ground between public and international schools. These schools teach the French national curriculum but also offer instruction in a second language, such as English. This option can help children become fluent in both languages and adapt more easily to the French education system.

3. Childcare Services

Childcare services in France are widely available, with options ranging from nurseries (crèches) and preschools (maternelles) to childminders (assistantes maternelles) and babysitters. Some employers also offer childcare services or subsidies as part of their employee benefits package. To access public childcare services, you must be registered with the French social security system and have a valid work contract or be actively seeking employment.

4. Transportation Services

France has an extensive and efficient transportation system that includes trains, buses, trams, and metro services. In urban areas, public transportation is widely available, making it easy to get around without a car. Outside of cities, a personal vehicle may be necessary, as public transportation options can be more limited.

a. Trains

The French national railway company, SNCF, operates an extensive network of high-speed (TGV), regional (TER), and suburban (Transilien) trains. Train travel in France is comfortable, reliable, and relatively affordable, especially when booked in advance. Discounted fares are available for children, young adults, seniors, and frequent travelers.

b. Buses, Trams, and Metro

Most French cities and towns have a comprehensive bus network, while larger cities like Paris, Lyon, and Marseille also have tram and metro systems. Public transportation is generally affordable, with various ticket options and discount passes available.

c. Taxis and Ridesharing

Taxis and ridesharing services like Uber are available in most cities and towns. However, they can be more expensive than public transportation. It's essential to ensure that you use a licensed taxi or a reputable ridesharing app to avoid scams or safety issues.

5. Utilities and Telecommunications

In France, utilities such as electricity, gas, and water are typically not included in rental agreements and must be set up separately. Providers include EDF (electricity), Engie (gas), and Veolia (water). For telecommunications, including internet, landline, and mobile phone services, there are several major providers, such as Orange, SFR, Bouygues, and Free. Bundled packages, known as "box" offers, are common and can save you money by combining multiple services.

6. Banking and Finance

Opening a French bank account is essential for managing your finances, receiving your salary, and paying bills. There are several national banks, such as BNP Paribas, Société Générale, and Crédit Agricole, as well as online banks like N26 or Revolut. To open an account, you will generally need proof of identity, proof of address, and an employment contract or proof of income.

By understanding and accessing these services, you can ensure that you and your family have the support you need to thrive in France.

□

VIII: RENOVATIONS AND PROPERTY MANAGEMENT

Owning a property in France is an exciting venture, but it also comes with responsibilities, such as renovations and property management. This chapter will guide you through the essential aspects of maintaining your French home, from navigating the renovation process to understanding property management services. By mastering these elements, you can ensure your property remains in excellent condition and becomes a valuable investment, whether you plan to live in it full-time or rent it out to others. Let's dive into the world of renovations and property management in France!

HIRING CONTRACTORS AND NAVIGATING FRENCH BUILDING REGULATIONS

When renovating a property in France, hiring the right contractors and understanding the local building regulations are crucial to ensuring a successful and hassle-free project. This section will provide guidance on finding reliable professionals and navigating the French building codes to ensure your property renovations meet the necessary standards.

1. Finding Contractors

Finding trustworthy and skilled contractors is an essential step in any renovation project. To find reputable professionals, consider the following strategies:

• **Personal Recommendations**: Ask for recommendations from friends, neighbors, or colleagues who have completed similar projects in the area. This approach can help you find contractors who have a proven track record and come highly recommended by people you trust.

• **Online Research**: Search online for local contractors and read reviews from previous clients to gauge their reputation and quality of work. Websites like artisans-trouver.fr or travaux.com can be useful in finding professionals in your area.

• **Local Directory**: Consult a local directory, such as Pages Jaunes (French Yellow Pages), to find listings for contractors in your area. Keep in mind that it's essential to conduct further research on any professionals you find through this method.

2. Obtaining Quotes

Before hiring a contractor, it's important to obtain several quotes (devis) to compare prices and services. When requesting a quote, make sure to provide a detailed description of your project and ask the contractor to itemize the costs for labor, materials, and any additional fees. This level of detail will help you make an informed decision when selecting a contractor.

3. Signing a Contract

Once you have chosen a contractor, it's crucial to sign a written contract (contrat) outlining the scope of work, costs, payment schedule, and expected completion date. A well-drafted contract can help protect your interests and minimize potential disputes during the renovation process.

4. Understanding French Building Regulations

Navigating French building regulations is essential to ensuring your renovation project complies with local standards and avoids any legal issues. Below are some key aspects of French building codes to consider:

• **Planning Permission**: For significant renovations or alterations, such as extensions or changes to the building's structure, you may need planning permission (permis de construire) from the local town hall (mairie). Smaller projects may only require a declaration of work (déclaration préalable). Consult with your contractor or local authorities to determine the necessary permits for your project.

• **Architect Involvement**: For projects exceeding a certain size (150 square meters), French law requires the involvement of a registered architect (architecte). The architect will help ensure your project complies with local regulations and can assist with obtaining the necessary permits.

• **Energy Efficiency:** France has stringent energy efficiency regulations (Réglementation Thermique) that apply to renovation projects. Depending on the scope of your project, you may be required to upgrade insulation, heating systems, or other elements to meet these standards.

• **Heritage Protection:** If your property is located in a protected area or is classified as a historic building, additional regulations may apply. Be sure to consult with your contractor, architect, or local authorities to determine any specific requirements for your property.

Hiring reliable contractors and understanding French building regulations are essential components of a successful renovation project. By thoroughly researching professionals, obtaining multiple quotes, signing a written contract, and navigating the necessary permits and regulations, you can ensure your property renovation goes smoothly and enhances the value of your French home.

□

ESTIMATING RENOVATION COSTS AND TIMELINES

Undertaking a renovation project in France can be an exciting way to transform your property into your dream home or increase its value. However, it's crucial to have a clear understanding of the costs and timelines involved to ensure the project proceeds smoothly and within budget. This section will provide guidance on estimating renovation expenses and setting realistic expectations for project timelines.

1. Determining the Scope of Work

Before estimating costs and timelines, it's essential to define the scope of your renovation project. Make a list of the work you want to be done, including both essential improvements and desirable upgrades. This list will help you prioritize tasks and allocate your budget accordingly.

2. Researching Average Costs

To get a rough idea of the costs involved in your renovation project, research average prices for the various tasks on your list. Keep in mind that costs can vary depending on factors such as regional differences, property size, and the quality of materials used. Online resources, like travaux.com, can provide an overview of average costs for different types of renovation work in France.

3. Requesting Detailed Quotes

Once you have a general sense of the costs involved, request detailed quotes from multiple contractors to compare their services and prices accurately. Make sure the quotes include a breakdown of the costs for labor, materials, and any additional fees, such as permits or waste disposal.

When reviewing quotes, remember that the cheapest option is not always the best choice. Assess the quality of the contractor's previous work, their reputation, and their ability to complete your project within your desired timeline.

4. Budgeting for Contingencies

Renovation projects often involve unforeseen expenses, such as additional repairs, unexpected delays, or changes to the original plan. To account for these uncertainties, add a contingency allowance of 10-20% to your estimated renovation budget. This cushion will help you cover any unexpected costs without jeopardizing the project's completion.

5. Estimating Timelines

Setting realistic expectations for your renovation project's timeline is essential to avoid disappointment or financial strain. While it's natural to want the work completed as quickly as possible, it's important to recognize that renovations often take longer than initially anticipated.

To estimate a realistic timeline for your project, consider the following factors:

• The scope of work: Larger, more complex projects will typically require more time to complete. Factor in the time it takes to obtain permits, order materials, and coordinate with multiple contractors.

• Contractor availability: Depending on the time of year and the local market, contractors may be booked months in advance. Make sure to factor in potential delays when scheduling your renovation project.

• Unforeseen issues: Renovation projects can uncover hidden issues, such as structural damage or outdated wiring, which can extend the project's timeline. Ensure that your schedule allows for some flexibility to address any unexpected challenges.

• Weather and seasonal factors: Some renovation tasks, such as exterior work, may be weather-dependent. Be prepared for potential delays due to adverse conditions or seasonal factors.

6. Monitoring Progress

During the renovation process, maintain regular communication with your contractor to stay informed about the project's progress and address any issues that arise. Keeping a close eye on the project will help you ensure it stays on track, both in terms of budget and timeline.

Accurately estimating renovation costs and timelines is crucial for a successful project. By researching average costs, obtaining detailed quotes, budgeting for contingencies, and setting realistic expectations for timelines, you can effectively manage your renovation project and achieve your desired outcome.

FINDING PROPERTY MANAGERS AND CARETAKERS

Whether you plan to live in your French property full-time or use it as a holiday home or rental investment, effective property management is essential to maintaining its value and ensuring it runs smoothly. Hiring a property manager or caretaker can take the stress out of managing your home from afar or juggling the day-to-day tasks of property maintenance. This section will guide you through the process of finding the right property management professionals to suit your needs.

1. Understanding the Roles of Property Managers and Caretakers

Before beginning your search, it's essential to understand the different roles property managers and caretakers play in maintaining your property. Property managers typically oversee rental properties, handle tenant relations, and manage the financial and administrative aspects of property ownership. In contrast, caretakers are responsible for the day-to-day maintenance and upkeep of a property, such as gardening, cleaning, and minor repairs.

Depending on your needs, you may require the services of one or both types of professionals. Consider your property's intended use and your available time and resources when determining which services best suit your situation.

2. Searching for Property Managers and Caretakers

To find reliable property managers and caretakers, consider the following strategies:

• Personal Recommendations: Ask for referrals from friends, neighbors, or colleagues who own property in the area. This approach can help you find professionals who come highly recommended and have a proven track record.

• Online Research: Conduct an online search for local property management companies or caretakers, and read reviews from previous clients to gauge their reputation and quality of service. Websites like bienici.com or seloger.com can be useful in finding property management professionals in your area.

• Local Directory: Consult a local directory, such as Pages Jaunes (French Yellow Pages), to find listings for property management companies and caretakers in your area. Remember to conduct further research on any professionals you find through this method.

3. Interviewing Candidates

Once you have identified potential property managers and caretakers, schedule interviews to assess their suitability for your needs. During the interview, consider the following factors:

• Experience and qualifications: Ask about their experience managing properties similar to yours, as well as any relevant qualifications or certifications they hold.

• Services provided: Discuss the specific services they offer and ensure they align with your property's requirements. For property managers, inquire about their tenant screening process, rent collection methods, and maintenance procedures. For caretakers, ask about their availability, areas of expertise, and any additional services they can provide, such as emergency repairs or seasonal maintenance.

• Fees and contract terms: Discuss their fees and contract terms, including any additional costs for services not included in their base rate. Ensure you have a clear understanding of the services provided and the associated costs before signing a contract.

• Communication and rapport: Gauge their communication style and ability to establish a rapport with you. Effective communication is essential for successful property management, especially if you will be managing the property remotely.

4. Checking References

Before hiring a property manager or caretaker, request and check references from previous clients to verify their reliability, professionalism, and quality of service. This step can provide valuable insight into their work ethic and ability to meet your property management needs.

5. Signing a Contract

Once you have selected a property manager or caretaker, sign a written contract outlining the scope of services, fees, and terms of the agreement. A well-drafted contract can help protect your interests and ensure both parties have a clear understanding of their roles and responsibilities.

6. Ongoing Communication and Management

After hiring a property manager or caretaker, maintain regular communication to stay informed about your property's status and address any issues that arise. Establish a communication schedule and preferred method, such as email updates, phone calls, or video conferences, to ensure you stay in the loop and can make informed decisions.

7. Evaluating Performance and Adjusting Services

Periodically evaluate the performance of your property manager or caretaker to ensure they are meeting your expectations and delivering quality service. Consider factors such as their responsiveness to your inquiries, their ability to resolve issues promptly, and the overall condition of your property.

If you find that your property management professional is not meeting your expectations, discuss your concerns with them and explore options for improving their performance. This may involve adjusting the scope of their services, renegotiating fees, or, if necessary, seeking a new property manager or caretaker.

8. Building a Long-Term Relationship

A successful property management relationship is built on trust, communication, and mutual understanding. By treating your property manager or caretaker with respect, recognizing their expertise, and collaborating on decisions, you can foster a positive working relationship that benefits both parties.

Remember to express appreciation for their efforts and acknowledge their hard work, as this can go a long way in building rapport and encouraging their continued dedication to your property. Additionally, consider providing performance-based incentives, such as bonuses or increased fees, to reward their efforts and motivate them to maintain a high level of service.

Finding and working with the right property manager or caretaker is vital to the successful maintenance and management of your French property. By following the steps outlined above, you can identify, hire, and build a strong working relationship with a property management professional who meets your needs and helps you achieve your property ownership goals.

UNDERSTANDING FRENCH RENTAL LAWS AND OPPORTUNITIES

Renting out your French property can be a rewarding and lucrative investment, but it's essential to understand the local rental laws and regulations to ensure a smooth experience for both you and your tenants. This section will provide an overview of the French rental market and the legal framework governing rental properties, as well as discuss the opportunities available to property owners.

1. Overview of the French Rental Market

The French rental market is diverse and dynamic, with a mix of long-term and short-term rentals catering to various tenant needs. In urban areas, there is strong demand for rental properties, particularly in popular cities like Paris, Lyon, and Marseille. Meanwhile, in rural and coastal regions, holiday rentals are prevalent, offering property owners the opportunity to capitalize on the tourism industry.

Before renting out your property, it's crucial to research the local rental market and understand the demand, rental rates, and tenant preferences to maximize your investment's potential.

2. Legal Framework for Rental Properties in France

French rental laws are designed to protect both landlords and tenants and provide a framework for their relationship. The primary legislation governing rental properties in France is the "Loi Alur" (Law for Access to Housing and Urban Renovation), which was enacted in 2014 and has since been amended several times. The key aspects of this law relevant to property owners include:

• Security deposit: Landlords can require a security deposit equivalent to one month's rent for unfurnished rentals and two months' rent for furnished rentals. The deposit must be returned to the tenant within one month after the end of the lease, minus any deductions for damages or unpaid rent.

• Rent control: In some areas, such as Paris and Lille, rent control regulations limit the amount landlords can charge for rental properties. Landlords must adhere to these limits, which are based on factors such as location, property size, and age.

• Lease terms: The minimum lease term for unfurnished rentals is three years, while furnished rentals require a minimum lease of one year. Short-term holiday rentals are subject to different regulations, which are discussed in more detail below.

• Tenant eviction: Evicting a tenant in France can be a complex and lengthy process, requiring adherence to specific procedures and timelines. Landlords must provide a valid reason for eviction, such as non-payment of rent or breach of the lease terms, and must give the tenant proper notice.

3. Types of Rental Properties in France

There are several types of rental properties available to property owners in France, each with its unique set of regulations and opportunities:

• Long-term rentals: These rentals are intended for tenants who plan to reside in the property for an extended period, typically ranging from one to several years. Long-term rentals can be either furnished or unfurnished and are subject to the lease terms and rent control regulations outlined above.

• Short-term holiday rentals: Popular in tourist destinations, these rentals cater to vacationers and typically range from a few days to several weeks. Short-term holiday rentals are subject to specific regulations under the French "Loi Elan" (Evolution of Housing, Development, and Digital Technology Law), which requires property owners to register their rental with the local municipality and adhere to a maximum annual rental limit (120 days in some areas).

• Seasonal rentals: Similar to short-term holiday rentals, seasonal rentals cater to tourists but are typically rented out for a specific season, such as summer or winter. Seasonal rentals are subject to the same regulations as short-term holiday rentals but may offer additional opportunities for property owners to capitalize on peak tourist seasons

4. Opportunities for Property Owners

Renting out your French property can offer several benefits and opportunities, including:

• Rental income: By renting out your property, you can generate a steady stream of rental income to offset your expenses and potentially earn a profit. Depending on the location, type of property, and rental market conditions, the return on investment can be significant.

• Capital appreciation: In addition to rental income, owning a property in France can lead to capital appreciation as the value of the property increases over time. This can be especially advantageous in areas with high demand and limited supply, such as popular tourist destinations or major cities.

• Tax benefits: Renting out your property can offer certain tax advantages, such as deductions for rental-related expenses and the ability to offset rental income against property-related costs. It's essential to consult with a tax professional familiar with French tax laws to understand the specific benefits and requirements that apply to your situation.

• Diversification: Renting out your French property can be an excellent way to diversify your investment portfolio by adding real estate assets to your holdings. This can help spread risk and potentially increase your overall returns.

• Personal use: One of the benefits of owning a rental property in France is the ability to use it for your own vacations or extended stays. By carefully planning your rental calendar and reserving time for your personal use, you can enjoy the best of both worlds – generating rental income while also having a place to call home in France.

5. Managing Your Rental Property

Successfully managing a rental property in France requires careful planning, attention to detail, and adherence to local laws and regulations. Some key aspects to consider include:

• Marketing and advertising: To attract tenants and maximize your rental income, it's important to market your property effectively. This can involve listing your property on popular rental websites, working with local estate agents, and using social media and other marketing tools to reach potential tenants.

• Tenant screening: Finding reliable and responsible tenants is crucial for a successful rental property. Conduct thorough background checks, request references, and verify income and employment information to ensure that your prospective tenants are a good fit for your property.

• Property maintenance: Regular maintenance and upkeep are essential to keep your rental property in good condition and attract quality tenants. This includes routine tasks such as cleaning, repairs, and landscaping, as well as larger projects such as renovations or upgrades.

• Legal compliance: As a landlord, it's your responsibility to ensure that your rental property complies with all applicable laws and regulations. This includes obtaining the necessary permits, registering your rental with the local municipality (if required), and adhering to local rental and tax laws.

• Professional support: Managing a rental property can be complex, particularly if you're not familiar with the local laws and customs or don't live nearby. Consider hiring a property manager or working with a local estate agent to help you navigate the process and ensure a successful rental experience.

Renting out your French property can be a rewarding and profitable venture, provided you understand the local rental laws and seize the opportunities available to you. By carefully managing your property, complying with regulations, and staying attuned to market trends, you can make the most of your investment and enjoy the benefits of owning a rental property in France.

IX: THE JOURNEY TO YOUR DREAM HOME IN FRANCE

As we reach the end of this comprehensive guide, it's time to reflect on the journey you've taken to learn about the ins and outs of buying a property in France. From understanding the appeal of the French lifestyle and culture to navigating the legal framework and financial considerations, you have acquired the knowledge necessary to make informed decisions and maximize your investment.

In this concluding chapter, we will recap the essential points covered throughout the book, providing you with a concise summary of the key aspects to consider when purchasing a home in France. We will also explore the ongoing responsibilities of property ownership and discuss the importance of adapting to and embracing the local culture and customs.

With this foundation, you can now confidently embark on your own adventure of finding and acquiring your dream property in France. By applying the insights, strategies, and tips provided in this guide, you can navigate the home buying process with ease, making the experience both enjoyable and rewarding.

EMBRACING YOUR NEW LIFE IN FRANCE

As you settle into your new home in France, it's essential to embrace the unique lifestyle, culture, and customs that make this country so special. By immersing yourself in French life and integrating into the local community, you'll create a fulfilling and enriching experience that will truly make you feel at home. Here are some key aspects to consider as you begin your new life in France.

1. Language and Communication

Learning French is crucial for a smooth transition to your new life in France. A basic understanding of the language will help you navigate everyday situations, from shopping at the local market to interacting with neighbors and making friends. Invest time and effort in learning French, either through language classes, online courses, or language exchange programs. As your proficiency improves, you'll find it easier to communicate with locals, understand cultural nuances, and appreciate the beauty of the French language.

2. Cultural Immersion

Take time to explore and experience the rich and diverse culture of France. Attend local events, festivals, and exhibitions to gain a deeper understanding of the country's history, art, and traditions. Visit museums, galleries, and historical sites to appreciate the depth of French heritage. By actively participating in local cultural activities, you'll develop a greater appreciation for your new home and forge stronger connections with the local community.

3. Building Relationships

Establishing a social network is an essential aspect of integrating into French society. Make an effort to meet and engage with your neighbors, local shopkeepers, and community members. Attend social gatherings, join clubs or interest groups, and volunteer for community events or initiatives. Building relationships with the people around you will not only help you feel more connected but also provide valuable support and resources as you navigate your new life in France.

4. Embracing French Cuisine

France is renowned for its exquisite cuisine, and embracing this aspect of French culture will enrich your daily life. Discover the joys of French cooking by visiting local markets, where you can buy fresh, seasonal produce and learn about regional specialties. Attend cooking classes or workshops to master the art of French cuisine and incorporate it into your everyday meals. Dining out at local restaurants will introduce you to a wide variety of culinary experiences, from traditional bistro fare to Michelin-starred gastronomy.

5. Adapting to French Etiquette and Customs

Understanding and adapting to French etiquette and customs will help you integrate more easily into your new community. Some essential aspects to consider include:

• Politeness: The French place a strong emphasis on politeness in social interactions. Always greet people with a polite "Bonjour" (hello) and address them by their title (Monsieur, Madame) followed by their last name.

• Dress code: In general, the French dress more formally than in many other countries. Dressing appropriately for different occasions and settings will show your respect for local customs and help you make a positive impression.

• Dining etiquette: French dining etiquette is more formal than in some other cultures. It's essential to learn and adhere to the basic rules, such as waiting for the host to begin eating, using utensils correctly, and not placing your elbows on the table.

By embracing the French way of life, you'll create a fulfilling and enjoyable experience as a new resident in this beautiful country. Integrating into the local community, learning the language, and adapting to the culture will not only make your transition smoother but also help you truly appreciate the essence of living in France.

□

ENJOYING THE REWARDS OF HOMEOWNERSHIP IN FRANCE

After navigating the complexities of the home buying process and settling into your new life in France, it's time to sit back and enjoy the many rewards that come with homeownership in this captivating country. From the personal satisfaction of owning your dream property to the long-term financial benefits of your investment, the advantages of owning a home in France are abundant. In this final chapter, we will explore the various aspects of homeownership that make the journey worthwhile and fulfilling.

1. Personal Fulfillment and Pride

One of the most significant rewards of homeownership in France is the personal fulfillment and pride that comes from owning a piece of this enchanting country. Whether you've purchased a charming village house, a countryside château, or a modern city apartment, your French property represents your hard work, perseverance, and commitment to turning your dream into reality.

As a homeowner, you can fully embrace the French lifestyle and create a home that reflects your unique tastes and preferences. From interior design and landscaping to renovations and additions, you have the freedom to shape your property into the perfect sanctuary, a place where you can build lasting memories and experiences with family and friends.

2. A Strong Sense of Community

Owning a home in France often comes with a strong sense of community, as you become an integral part of your local neighborhood or village. By attending local events, participating in community projects, and engaging with your neighbors, you will forge meaningful connections and relationships that will enrich your life.

In many French communities, there is a deep sense of history and tradition that creates a powerful bond between residents. As a homeowner, you become a custodian of this heritage, playing a vital role in preserving and nurturing the unique character of your community for future generations.

3. Long-term Financial Benefits

Owning a property in France can provide substantial long-term financial benefits. While the initial costs of purchasing and maintaining a property can be significant, homeownership often leads to increased wealth accumulation over time. As your property appreciates in value, you can build equity, which can then be leveraged for further investments, retirement planning, or other financial goals.

Additionally, owning a property in France can provide rental income opportunities. By renting out your home, either as a long-term lease or a short-term vacation rental, you can generate a steady stream of income to help offset the costs of homeownership or even turn a profit. This can be particularly beneficial for those who have purchased properties in popular tourist destinations or sought-after locations.

4. Tax Advantages

While taxes and fees associated with buying and owning property in France can be substantial, there are also several tax advantages available to homeowners. For example, certain renovations and energy-efficient upgrades can qualify for tax credits or deductions, helping to offset the costs of home improvements. Additionally, rental income from your property may be eligible for tax deductions or exemptions, depending on your specific situation and the type of rental arrangement.

It's essential to consult with a tax professional or financial advisor to ensure you fully understand and take advantage of any tax benefits applicable to your situation. By optimizing your tax strategy, you can further enhance the financial rewards of homeownership in France.

5. A Gateway to Europe

One of the most exciting aspects of owning a property in France is the country's central location within Europe. As a homeowner, you have a convenient base from which to explore the diverse cultures, landscapes, and experiences that Europe has to offer. Whether it's a weekend getaway to a neighboring country or a longer European adventure, your French home serves as a gateway to a world of travel and exploration.

6. A Refuge and Retreat

In today's fast-paced world, having a place to escape the stresses of daily life and find tranquility is more important than ever. Your French property can serve as a refuge and retreat, a place where you can disconnect, recharge, and find inspiration. The diverse landscapes and natural beauty of France provide the perfect backdrop for relaxation, from the serene countryside and picturesque vineyards to the breathtaking coastlines and majestic mountains.

By cultivating a garden, engaging in outdoor activities, or simply enjoying the peaceful ambiance of your surroundings, your French home can become a sanctuary for your physical and emotional well-being.

7. Immersion in French Culture

Homeownership in France offers you the opportunity to fully immerse yourself in French culture, allowing you to embrace and appreciate the customs, traditions, and values that make the country so unique. From savoring the delights of French cuisine and wine to exploring the rich history and artistic heritage, your life as a homeowner in France will be infused with cultural experiences that will enrich and enlighten you.

By participating in local festivals, attending cultural events, and supporting local artisans, you will become an active participant in French culture, fostering a deeper connection to your new home and the people who share it with you.

8. A Lasting Legacy

Purchasing a property in France can also be seen as an investment in your family's future, creating a lasting legacy for generations to come. As a homeowner, you have the opportunity to pass down your property to your children or other family members, ensuring that the joys and benefits of homeownership in France continue to be experienced by those you love.

By instilling a love for French culture, fostering connections to the community, and creating cherished memories, your French property will become a meaningful and enduring part of your family's story.

9. Building a Network of Support

As you navigate the challenges and joys of homeownership in France, you will inevitably build a network of support, including fellow expats, local friends, and professionals in various fields. This network can be an invaluable resource, providing guidance, assistance, and camaraderie as you settle into your new life.

From sharing tips and advice to collaborating on projects and social events, your network of support will be an essential component of your success and satisfaction as a homeowner in France.

10. A Sense of Accomplishment

Finally, the process of buying a home in France, adapting to a new culture, and becoming a part of a community is a journey that requires determination, resilience, and courage. Successfully navigating this journey and achieving your dream of homeownership in France is a remarkable accomplishment, one that should be celebrated and cherished.

By embracing the rewards of homeownership in France, you can create a fulfilling and enriching life that is a testament to your hard work, dedication, and passion for this captivating country.

IN CONCLUSION

As we reach the end of this comprehensive guide, we hope that the information and insights provided have equipped you with the knowledge and confidence necessary to successfully navigate the complex world of buying a house in France. From understanding the nuances of the French property market to embracing the rewards of homeownership, this journey is both challenging and immensely rewarding.

Remember that the path to your dream home in France is a unique one, shaped by your individual preferences, goals, and circumstances. Be patient, stay focused, and maintain a positive outlook throughout the process. The challenges you encounter will ultimately lead to the fulfillment of your dreams, and the incredible experiences and memories that await you in your new French home.

As you embark on this exciting adventure, remember that you are not alone. A network of professionals, fellow expats, and supportive locals are there to assist and guide you, ensuring that you have the resources and encouragement necessary to succeed.

In conclusion, we wish you the best of luck as you pursue your dream of homeownership in France. May this experience be filled with growth, discovery, and joy, leading you to a life of unparalleled richness and fulfillment in the enchanting landscapes of this remarkable country.

Bonne chance et bon voyage!

ABOUT THE AUTHOR

Alistair McLeod, originally from the UK, is a seasoned real estate expert and author with 15 years of experience in Croatia's beautiful Istria region. His expertise in international real estate and personal expatriate experiences equip him with unique insights into the challenges and rewards of buying property and starting a new life abroad.

Author of successful books on buying homes in Croatia and Italy, his latest offering, The Ultimate Guide to Buying a House in France, provides an in-depth analysis of the French property market, legal framework, and cultural nuances. When not writing or assisting clients, Alistair's passion for travel and local culture further enhances his credentials as the perfect guide for potential homeowners in France.

Visit his website at www.alistairmcleod.com or reach out directly at info@alistairmcleod.com

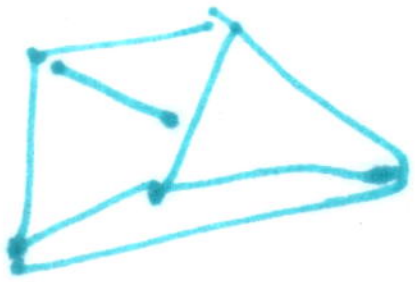

Printed in Great Britain
by Amazon

46097677R00096